PRAISE FOR *NINETEEN*

"This father's powerful testimonial to his son captures both the pain of loss and the joys of life. It invites us to pause in this hectic world, to appreciate it and those around us. It is not a story of despair but that of love. These thought-provoking pages will act as a source of strength for those who knew Haydn Robarts and those that did not. Through his work, Adam Robarts has offered others the chance to know the man I was lucky enough to call my friend."

—*Chris George, Haydn's school friend*

"This book, like the life of the one it tells, is full of deep wisdom and insight. Adam Robarts has given all who have the privilege of reading it a priceless gift: out of personal pain and heartbreaking loss, he has brought forth a message of triumph and transcendence. With him, we stand in awe of the life of nineteen-year-old Haydn Robarts, who speaks to our hearts, "Grieve not for me for I have indeed reached the summit, and the view from eternity is glorious.'"

—*Tarrant Mahony, Haydn's neighbor and Temple University professor of law at Tsinghua University, Beijing*

"This story is powerful in its powerlessness, graceful in its humility, and uplifting in its heartbreak. It breathes like a memoir or a self-help book, but this is really a love story. It is through this love that lessons are learned and a light emerges to guide us on our own spiritual path."

—*Karyn Robarts, Haydn's mother*

NINETEEN

Haydn with parents Karyn and Adam Robarts, New York; January 2020. *Photo courtesy of Pan Shiyi*

NINETEEN

19 Insights Learned
from a 19-year-old with Cancer

ADAM J. T. ROBARTS

with Karen Malmqvist
and Lou Aronica

LEO | **Regan Arts.**

Regan Arts paperback edition, May 2022
1 3 5 7 9 10 8 6 4 2

Library of Congress Control Number: 2021949934

ISBN 978-1-68245-200-4 (Paperback)
ISBN 978-1-68245-201-1 (Ebook)

Interior design by Pauline Neuwirth, Neuwirth & Associates
Cover design by Richard Ljoenes
Mountain range photo by iStock.com/fbxx

Printed in the United States of America

This book is dedicated to Haydn's siblings:
Tallis, Sian, and Keyan.

May Haydn always inspire you to live your lives as he would wish, "for the betterment of the world," with hearts filled with joy, and consciously bringing joy to others.

To my parents and grandparents

CONTENTS

mapping the mountain

CONTENTS

the summit

reflections on descent

NINETEEN

mapping the mountain

1.

HAYDN'S PATH

––––––––––––––––––––

THREE AND A HALF YEARS BEFORE THIS STORY BEGAN, HAYDN AND I made a three-day trip from our Beijing home to Wellington College in the UK. Haydn had been invited to sit for the entrance exam for Wellington's sixth form, equivalent to an American twelfth grade, where four hundred applicants vied for forty places. Jet-lagged but excited, we stood waiting in the school reception hall with the other candidates and their parents. Smiles and small talk disguised the nervousness among us before our fifteen-year-olds were led off to their first exam of the day: mathematics. As they parted, a Russian boy standing within earshot spoke quietly to his father, checking off his exam tools: pen, pencil, geometry set, calculator. Haydn turned to me and calmly said, "Dad, I didn't bring my calculator." My heart skipped a beat. Just as instantly, and true to form, Haydn assured me with his characteristic calm, "Don't worry. It'll be okay." Without hesitation, Haydn chose grace in the face of challenge.

In mid-July 2019, then nineteen-year-old Haydn, my always hale son, started experiencing headaches, blurred vision, and some nausea. He didn't look sick at all, however. He was in Toronto, having just finished his gap year in China and Chile, following sixth form at Wellington. A few weeks later, he was due to start studying architecture at University College London with a focus on sustainable architecture. Here stood a young man at the trailhead of his future, dreams and exciting plans intact, the course laid out. But the physical anomalies he was experiencing demanded attention.

At the advice of my brother, an ER doctor, Haydn went in for an MRI, just to be safe. That August 1, I was in Singapore in a hotel room with my wife, Karyn, and our youngest son, Keyan. We were preparing to fly to our new home in Bali later that afternoon. Keyan was excited to begin his schooling near Ubud. So, there we stood, also poised at the trailhead of a new journey. This was an exciting beginning for us, and we were positive and optimistic about everything that awaited us on the Island of the Gods.

Then the phone rang.

My brother broke the news to us: Haydn's MRI showed a tumor four centimeters in diameter beside the pituitary gland, at the base of the brain. He needed emergency surgery as he was already losing his eyesight and hearing, and his speech had begun to slur.

I was confused and shocked. When I'd last seen Haydn, only three weeks earlier, he appeared in fine health, perhaps in better shape than ever before.

In that drop-to-your-knees moment, our world seemed to crumble around us and within us. Karyn and I held each other and just wept and wept . . . and wept. Disoriented, stunned, and scared, we suddenly stood at a new trailhead, the destination and the routes completely unknown. We quickly gathered our wits, booked tickets, and flew to Toronto on the next flight.

> *One of the ego's many erroneous assumptions, one of its many deluded thoughts is, "I should not have to suffer." Sometimes the thought gets transferred to someone close to you: "My child should not have to suffer." That thought itself lies at the root of suffering. . . . The truth is that you need to say yes to suffering before you can transcend it.*
>
> —ECKHART TOLLE, *A New Earth*

Haydn's cancer treatments in Toronto consisted of two brain sur-geries followed by twelve weeks of chemotherapy and a subsequent eight weeks of radiation treatments. At the time of his diagnosis, Haydn's bloodwork showed that his alpha-fetoprotein (AFP), one of several tumor markers, was extremely elevated. The normal range for AFP is less than 3 ng/mL (nanograms per milliliter), and Haydn's AFP was at 8,500 ng/mL when he started chemotherapy. Twelve weeks later, at the end of chemo, it was down to 25 ng/mL. At the same time, the high-resolution brain scans showed that Haydn's brain tumor had reduced from four centimeters to seven millimeters in diameter. A reduction in diameter by a factor of six translates to a reduction in volume by almost 200 times. We were all elated! With thirty-three sessions of radiation still to come, it seemed we had wind in our sails, and were set to enter remission at the end of this journey. The year 2020 was looking to be a good one.

If all went according to plan, Haydn's last radiation treatment would be January 6, 2020, and we would mark it as the summit of his journey through cancer. We envisioned this to be a brief detour be-fore returning to a normal, healthy life. However, on January 7, Haydn's blood work showed his AFP level at 1151 ng/mL. Some-thing wasn't right. The oncologists were clearly concerned and want-ed to first verify that this was not a mistake. They booked additional blood work as well as high resolution MRI scans of Haydn's head and spine. Three days later, we met with the oncologists for the ver-dict: Haydn's cancer had spread from his brain to his spine and was resistant to the treatment. This was a rare and aggressive form of cancer, and the odds of a cure were not hopeful. The doctors deter-mined that Haydn's condition had progressed too far, and since he'd been unresponsive to treatment, they concluded that no fur-ther treatment was viable.

In a small clinic room at the Princess Margaret Hospital on that ominous day, Haydn was told that he should just try to make the most of his remaining time in this earthly life, likely only a few months. The doctors were apologetic, sensitive, and professional. They informed Haydn that they would refer a palliative care team that would be able to support him through this final phase.

In that moment, Haydn was calm and collected. A few tears trickled down his cheeks as he processed the news. He straightened himself and thanked the doctors, genuinely, for he knew they had done their best. He asked what he could and couldn't do. Could he travel? Or skydive?! I sat deeply saddened and, frankly, numb. There were no tears or outbursts of disbelief or anger or guilt. I believed we did everything we could to prevent this outcome, yet that didn't make this news any less awful. Haydn then turned to Karyn, who had to lie down to manage the shock, as it left her physically breathless and faint. He gently put his hand on her shoulder and ever so lovingly assured her that all would be fine. When Haydn spoke, a gentle certitude filled the room. The simple sincerity of his words lifted us all.

Nothing I had ever read or learned or achieved adequately prepared me for this heartrending reality. While I try not to go back to this particular moment, Karyn has called upon it many times. She describes it as her proudest as a mother: when she witnessed the culmination of a character Haydn cultivated during his nineteen years that enabled him to accept his fate with such grace and gratitude. We know in our hearts that this journey revealed Haydn's depth of character, his fortitude, and a level of faith that I can describe only in words like profound, inspiring . . . heroic.

When we returned to the apartment after that momentous meeting with the doctors, Haydn wrote this personal message to family and friends:

Dear All,

I want to thank everyone in this email chain for being with me in spirit over the course of this journey. Your responses and just knowing that so many people are taking an interest in my well-being has been incredible!

The next few months will no doubt be difficult for me, and while I would appreciate any prayers for a miracle, I also ask that, if I am to meet a premature end, that you don't feel bad for me or my family, for everything happens for a reason.

I have lived an incredible life! Surrounded by constant love, support, and opportunities! It is a life I am extremely grateful for, and I couldn't have asked for a more supporting and loving family/group of friends to have around me!

boundless love,
Haydn

From the time of Haydn's diagnosis, I felt drawn to the metaphor of mountain climbing. During this climb, it seemed my relationship with Haydn shifted from being that of a father accompanying his son to more of a companion accompanying a young mountaineer scaling a formidable mountain. The grand teacher that is Mother Nature can redirect even the most well-equipped and well-trained climb team. When a storm suddenly moves in, questions immediately arise. Do conditions provide for a slight delay? If so, we look for a new window of opportunity to push to the top. Or is it best to surrender and call off the approach? Do we accept that this summit attempt was not meant to be?

For Haydn, giving up was not an option. At the same time, he was not one to force a situation, to push through a plan that was not viable. Haydn had the ability to bend, to flex, to give in rather than to give up. He believed that if God wanted him to make it through an illness, then there was a reason for his suffering, and he would channel that struggle into a purpose. And if God willed it that it was time for him to move on from this world, then Haydn also believed that he had a purpose in the next world for this exact time. Although he loved life, he had no fear of death. He accepted that there was a greater power at work in his life, whether one chooses to call it the Will of God, the Invisible Hand, fate, or destiny. Haydn often repeated the words of the thirteenth-century Persian poet Sa'di, quoted by Bahá'u'lláh in *Crisis and Victory,* to explain the operation of God's immutable Will and the effect on those who accept it:

Even or odd, thou shalt win the wager.

In the coming days, we sent out an SOS to all those we knew who might be able to introduce a lifeline. Were there any other possible routes, or teams? We researched proton beam therapy, biological treatments, and high-dose chemotherapy with stem cell rescue. We cast out a line to hospitals and pioneering centers in the UK, the US, Germany, South Korea, and China. If this was the end of the path, we wanted to be sure we had left no stone unturned. Even if the chances of success were slim, we never gave up hoping, believing, trusting. Miracles do happen, even in science. In fact, most scientific breakthroughs are described as miraculous by hard-nosed scientists who simply put their faith into being open to the miraculous.

Three days later, we were in communication with two leading cancer centers in the US, both in New York. Each were involved in a clinical trial for recurrent malignant tumors, including recurrent mixed germ-cell tumors. Haydn's case was presented at the tumor board meeting on Wednesday, January 15, 2020. Later that day, we were informed that an expert team at NYU was willing to take Haydn as a patient and would use high-dose chemotherapy with stem-cell rescue. The risks were evident, and there was no guarantee of success, but even though the odds were very low, Haydn was ready to give this climb everything he had. As he remarked one evening, even if there was a 1% chance of survival, that was 1% more than the option of giving up.

On January 17, exactly one week after being told the climb was over, we sat in Dr. Nicolaides' clinic in New York planning the schedule for Haydn's treatment. The conversation was surreal, yet very real. In less than six months, this was our second time round, in a second city, with a second set of doctors, looking at another cancer treatment plan. There was hope, but mine was now tempered given our previous experiences. I felt humbled and helpless by how little I could do medically for Haydn. Being conscious of my powerlessness, I was more mindful of everything else going on—the place, the people, the words spoken, my thoughts, my breathing . . . and, of course, the presence of Haydn. Somehow, he remained at ease, able to take it all in without being overwhelmed.

This plan involved an initial four rounds of chemotherapy, each lasting two weeks and involving different medications than those used in Toronto. If the cancer was responsive to this treatment, Haydn would move onto a course of myeloablative (literally "destroying the bone marrow") chemotherapy.

Stem-cell rescue entailed two phases, the first being to harvest the stem cells by extracting Haydn's blood from veins in his neck, running this through a centrifuge that would spin the blood to extract the stem cells, and then returning the blood to Haydn's body. Once Haydn's stem cells had been stored and frozen, the second phase would be to transplant the stem cells back into his body a couple of weeks later, after the myeloablative chemotherapy and the resulting depletion of all of Haydn's neutrophils and white blood cells. With the fresh stem cells starting a few days later to create new neutrophils and white blood cells, hopefully this would prompt a fresh start and a trail toward becoming cancer free. The procedure required precision timing and exactitude in handling, not least because Haydn would be highly immune compromised, with no defense against even the most minor of infections.

Haydn's first chemotherapy at NYU began on January 25; he was full of gratitude and hope as expressed in an email:

> *Thank you so much for your support, prayers, and beautiful replies to my dad's updates! I can't express how much it means to have such a wonderful support system in addition to my family and the incredibly capable team of doctors here!*
>
> *I'm feeling as well as can be expected and just incredibly grateful to*

have been given this treatment opportunity and for this glimmer of hope!
I'm ready to fight this thing, and with your unfailing support and
prayers, I believe God will give me the strength to do so! While I don't
necessarily "look forward" to the trials and difficulties that are sure to
come . . . I'm glad to have started treatment and I believe that no matter
what happens, there's a reason for it, and these difficulties will shape
not only myself to become a better person, but hopefully my family and
all of us :)

Again, thank you all for everything you've done for me during this
process, no matter how big or small ... be it taking enough of an interest
in my well-being to ask to be included in this email chain, sending
messages of love and support, or saying prayers for my recovery! I will
forever be grateful to you all!

Many thanks and boundless love!
Haydn

A week later, Haydn wrote, "Aside from some muscular aches and
stiffness, some persistent neuropathy, nausea, and lack of appetite,
things seem to have gone pretty well." Lying on his bed after a platelet transfusion, he added, "I seem to be getting used to IVs, so the
transfusions are becoming less and less daunting."

On February 10, Haydn began his second course of chemo in
New York. On February 19, his brain and spine MRI showed encouraging signs. The chemotherapy was definitely working. The letter we
received the following day from Haydn's oncologist gave us all a
boost of confidence and hope:

Compared to January 9, 2020:

Brain—The lesion in the pineal gland has shrunk by at least 20-
30% in volume. There remain some areas of tumor spread along the
surface of the brain.

Spine—The large lesion at T9 has shrunk by at least 50% and the
other areas of disease on the surface of the spine have shrunk significantly.

It is hard to know how much of this change is due to the radiation and how much due to the chemo. We do know that the AFP was rising when he came to us and is now decreasing, so for sure the chemo is contributing to the disease control.

As Haydn completed the first two trial courses of chemo with this heartening response to the treatment, doctors cleared him to continue with another two courses of chemo before the high-dose chemo and stem cell transplant. The third course of chemo was booked for Tuesday, February 25.

These results filled us with hope and reminded us of the book of Malachi, the last of the twelve Old Testament books that bear the names of the minor prophets. In it, there is a story of a refiner of silver. The refiner carefully works with the silver, burning off and scraping away the dross that the flames bring to the top. The silver is pure, and the refinement is complete, when the refiner looks into the open furnace or pot and can see his image plainly reflected in the molten metal. Without the heat, there is no refinement of silver. This seemed like an apt metaphor for our situation.

A week before Haydn's third course of chemo in New York, we learned about radiation somnolence syndrome, which often occurs six to eight weeks after radiation to the brain. We were unprepared for this, and we worried when Haydn was so sleepy, with headaches, nausea, and so little appetite that he hardly ate for six days. His counts were not quite high enough to begin the third course of chemo as scheduled, though he reached them two days later. A delay in getting the chemo ordered from the pharmacy pushed things back yet another day, and he started the third course of chemo at 9:00 a.m., February 28. For the Chinese, this is a lucky day, but was all going according to plan? Were the delays going to create another setback?

Naturally, terrains on mountains change as a climbing team pushes upward. Scree, or masses of loose rock, often covers a slope, creating a condition where climbers may take a couple of steps forward only to then slide back a step. When Haydn was being admitted to the hospital for his third course of chemo, he passed out. For the next nine days, he felt stable only when lying down. Hospitals don't discharge patients who aren't stable, so Haydn spent eight nights as an inpatient, after expecting to be there for one or two days at most. Two steps forward, one step back.

It was pure delight and relief when doctors discharged Haydn and he was able to go home, which involved walking up fourteen steps into the house! He spent that afternoon hanging out in the nook and eating. How great it was to see his appetite returning! After dinner that evening, Haydn climbed another seventeen steps to his bedroom. For someone who just two days earlier could hardly stand without feeling dizzy, this was a momentous feat.

In terms of the schedule, we were now in the recovery stage from chemo three. On March 12, Haydn was in the clinic for some repeat blood work when they discovered that his AFP levels had not dropped as expected. Instead, his AFP had risen a little. We knew this could be a sign that the tumors were becoming resistant to this regimen of chemotherapy. A step back. Again.

Given the apparent successes of the previous two months in New York, this news was very sobering. But Haydn took it with such grace and inner strength that we were, once again, inspired by his example. The doctors retested Haydn's AFP levels the following Monday and ordered repeat MRI scans of his brain and spine as well as another spinal tap to check the AFP levels there. By the end of that following week, everyone expected the tests to reveal a clearer picture of what was going on. At the same time, the medical team would be consulting with colleagues to see if there might be any other potentially viable treatments. From what I recall, those were days of ardent prayers and treasuring every single moment we had together. We knew what was at stake if the cancer had again become resistant to treatment. It was at that time that Karyn was sent this quotation attributed to Rúhíyyih Rabbání:

The sweetest flowers of man's spirit have most often been watered by tears. To struggle gives strength, to endure breeds a greater capacity for endurance. We must not run away from our heartbreaks in life; we must go through them, however fiery they may be, and bring with us out of the fire a stronger character, a deeper reliance on ourselves and on the Creator. . . .

We are not expected to like suffering; we should not foolishly think of it as some ascetics do, as a virtue in itself and cultivate it through self-mortification and torture; but we should when the cup is at our lips and we have no choice but to drink it, drink it down strongly and courageously, knowing it will hurt but strengthen, wound but eventually heal. Beauty can give joy, pain can give strength, sorrow can deepen the whole nature of a person. We must try to get out of every experience in life the very best it can offer.

This quote strengthened both Karyn and Haydn. They understood we never know which tests we might be given in our lives to endure. While this was by far our greatest test, we knew we needed to move with it to find meaning and light.

Haydn was a Bahá'í. However, he was also a devoted believer in science. I often observed how his love for science complimented his love for the Bahá'í Faith, which upholds the scientific method, whether in the laboratory or in spiritual search. Haydn struggled with being defined singularly as either a man of faith or a man of science and reason. Likewise, he struggled with being defined as either a man of arts or a man of sciences. His international baccalaureate diploma subjects were math, physics, English, Chinese, history, and art. Fortunately, the study of architecture at UCL offered a more integrated and holistic course that suited him well. Haydn's love for architecture was largely a love of integrated thinking and being, of integrated doing. In other words, of an integrated life. Even his tumor sat right in the midbrain, beside his pituitary gland, neither on the left nor on the right but in the perfect center. That was Haydn.

Those were interesting days in New York. COVID-19 had begun to spread throughout the city, most notably in Brooklyn, where we stayed. Getting from the apartment to the hospital entailed a long car ride or a short ferry ride across the East River. Haydn never took the ferry crossing because he was too weak by that point, and it was still cold and windy. However, the rest of us preferred to take the ferry to cross between the two stark worlds of hospital and home. It became a tonic to be on the water, the chilled wind blowing across one's face while the warm sunrays kissed rosy cheeks. I often thought about finding reconciliation and points of unity between the vivid contrasts we were all experiencing.

Those days we already wore masks. We watched as our daily accessory suddenly became a sweeping need around the globe as every day the number of COVID-19 cases climbed higher, especially in New York. Shops and restaurants started closing. America was getting the first winds of what would become a ravaging storm that would shake the country, and the world, with a deadly and highly contagious virus.

On Friday, March 20, I accompanied Haydn to the hospital for a relatively minor procedure. Because Haydn had such a rare tumor type, he had been asked a few days earlier whether some extra spinal fluid could be taken during the procedure for use in research. Haydn had, of course, agreed, always happy to advance science. If someone with the same tumor type had been able to do this in years past, maybe we would have known more about how to treat Haydn's condition.

When we arrived in the lobby of the hospital, we were met by a legion of masked and gowned receptionists, triage nurses, and security. It was day one of the new precautionary measures in hospitals across New York, and we were informed that I could not accompany Haydn beyond that point. This was hard to bear, as I was effectively Haydn's day nurse, with my bag containing his valuables, his meds, his water, and his urinal. I was the one who accompanied him to the washroom or helped him with those many tiny details of simply getting through each day. Imagine a mountain guide being told that only their mountaineer could proceed beyond a certain point. I must have looked blank and confused, or at least in slight disbelief, although I was ready to respect the safety protocols.

Thankfully, one of the receptionists looked up and said, "Hey, this guy is being treated as a pediatric patient, so he is allowed one family member to accompany him." What a relief! The barricade of gowns, gloves, and masks waved us through. Separating a frail and immunocompromised patient from the support and security of family, especially going into an unknown environment like COVID-19, is heartbreaking. Thankfully, we got only a taste of that possibility and were spared that anguish.

Two days later we received a call from Haydn's doctor. It was a beautiful and sunny Sunday morning, but the news was not encouraging. This is the email we sent afterward:

Dearest family and friends,

In these days of world-encompassing trials, we are thinking and praying for each of you and wish we could be closer! Here, we are celebrating the first days of spring and feel confident that this storm shall pass. While the immediate future may be dark, we take solace in faith that the distant future is surely brilliant.

We received a call from Haydn's doctor this morning to share that the AFP in the spinal fluid has increased quite significantly, and the medical team here has advised not to subject Haydn to further treatment. So, we are making plans to return on Wednesday to Ottawa, to our family home by a small lake near Wakefield. We will continue to pray for a possible miracle, and we are immensely grateful that you add your prayers to ours. The focus over the coming months will be to support Haydn to be able to have the best quality of life possible. He has an amazing inner strength and faith, so he is taking this direction with calm, grace, and hope that even dying, if that is the Will of God, can be a positive and beautiful process when supported by the love of family and friends and the mercy of the All-Merciful.

with heads held high and hearts full of hope,
AdamKarynTallisSianHaydnKeyan

We had prayed for clarity, that the doctors would provide us a path—and here it was—weighty, heart-wrenching, and life-changing.

As New Yorkers wondered what had hit them, we were realizing what had hit us. We needed time to process the depth of this devastating news, yet time was not on our side. We were unsure how much longer the borders would remain open to allow us back into Canada. Our phones began frantically ringing while we tried to keep calm and be present for one another and especially for Haydn. Occasionally, I would glance across at Haydn and think that he was really the eye of the hurricane, the calm at the center of our family storm. We had been blessed with a remarkable son who was solid and secure while the rest of us were buzzing around trying to organize returning the apartment, driving the car and our "stuff" across the border, and flying with Haydn—should he be approved to fly in his condition. One of the most surprising calls we received came from friends who insisted that they cover our costs to "fly private." God bless them! We needed to dash across the border during the chaotic dawn of what would become a confusing pandemic, with a frail and immunocompromised child. This was an extraordinarily thoughtful and generous gesture. To be picked up and driven to a waiting plane with no cramped security lines to wait in, no pushing and shoving at crowded baggage conveyor belts, and no flight delays was a gift beyond measure. And then, as if that wasn't enough to be grateful for, the same process happened at the other end: we were met at the plane and whisked away to our family cottage.

On March 25, we sent out a heartfelt email:

Dearest family and friends,

Thank you all for your love and prayers. We are today thankfully reunited at our home by a peaceful and beautiful little lake 25 mins north of Ottawa. Hard to imagine that a week ago we thought we would have been in the middle of stem-cell harvesting in a New York hospital. The hand of destiny in this journey has been mysterious— sometimes painful, sometimes beautiful, sometimes both—and we are filled with gratitude to be here right now. Today, Haydn is perhaps at the weakest we have seen. Tomorrow may be different.

love, prayers, hope, gratitude,
A

The six of us spent a poignant eight weeks at the lake house, learning about palliative care as we did our best to support our beloved Haydn during the last leg of his earthly journey. Those were our most difficult days. They were also our most rewarding.

Our family was tested beyond anything we had ever experienced before. Relationships were strained to breaking points, yet we all knew we had to pull together and make it through this ordeal. We surely owed it to Haydn to unite. This was not without its challenges. Most daunting, at least emotionally, was becoming amateur palliative care nurses. The real palliative care nurses were available only on Zoom, either because we were in quarantine or simply because nurses and doctors were suffering the demands of a strained healthcare system. As Haydn's steadfast climbing companions, we felt as if we stood alone on a spur, peering up the steepest ascent imaginable. How on earth would we scale this rock? It was well beyond our experience, yet none of us were about to turn around and descend. In fact, with this journey, there was no path back.

Haydn passed away in his bed at home, peacefully and surrounded by family, on May 19, 2020, one week before his twentieth birthday.

At the time of Haydn's diagnosis, I imagined and hoped with all my heart that conquering this disease would be akin to reaching a hard-earned summit. With his passing, I realized that Haydn did indeed reach the summit, just not in the way I imagined.

The following day we held a simple funeral and laid his earthly body to rest in a nearby cemetery, overlooking the hills and valleys north of Ottawa. The day after the funeral, we hosted a memorial gathering by Zoom that was attended by nearly a thousand family members and friends from all over the world. Many of them were young people, peers, and friends of Haydn's, whose tributes to his life didn't leave a dry eye.

—⁂—

Haydn kept phone notes and a little black notebook beside his bed where he listed ideas for a book he intended to write entitled *Why the "Self" in "Self-Help" Is Unimportant.* That would certainly have rattled an industry! I imagine he would find it amusing that his father subsequently chose to write a self-help book of sorts.

The first note on Haydn's list was "use quotes from all religions." This is of no surprise. Haydn's faith was central to his being, understated and with total acceptance of others and their viewpoints. So, with respect to Haydn, all of the chapters that follow begin with a selection of quotations from sacred scriptures, whether from the ancient wisdom of Hinduism and Buddhism, or from the Judeo-Christian religions of Judaism, Christianity, and Islam, or from the more recent scriptures of the Bahá'í Faith. Religion in this book is defined in a broad context as the investigation of reality, particularly spiritual reality. Quotations from the world's scriptures are therefore offered here to turn on a light at the start of each lesson, like a collection of stars that light the path ahead.

During his short life, and especially through his journey with cancer, Haydn made his contribution to this planet and especially to his generation. He added hope and love in the face of hopelessness and loss. We continue to receive news of people, particularly youth, inspired by Haydn's genuine desire to contribute to the betterment of the world. In Haydn's name, they have initiated service projects, from simple children's classes and junior youth activities for the environment, to memorial gardens in two of the schools he attended. Some of these people are family and close friends of Haydn, yet others never met him. Like Haydn, some are Bahá'ís, but others may never have heard the word. They simply share in a common goodness and a desire for role models and practical examples of what can be done to better the world.

It may be hard to see the end in the beginning, or to see around ominous precipices. Hindsight offers mighty lessons, and one of those is that even a calamity can be a gift from life, bringing with it light and hope. It is on us to be calm, agile, and open enough to accept it.

preparation
to climb

From acceptance, the disciple gains happiness supreme. One of the wise has said: accept conditions, accept others, accept yourself. This is the true acceptance, for all these things are what they are through the will of the higher Self, except their deficiencies, which come through thwarting the will of the higher Self and can be conquered only through compliance with that will.

—The Yoga Sutras of Patanjali, 2.95

Hear, sirs, a single word from me. Our Buddha's teaching was acceptance.

—Dīghanikāya: Long Discourses, XVI:39.10

Bestow upon me my portion, O Lord, as Thou pleasest, and cause me to be satisfied with whatsoever Thou hast ordained for me.

—Selections from the Writings of the Báb, 7.24.4

2.

ACCEPTANCE

"You get what you get, and you don't get upset."

HAYDN'S MIDDLE SCHOOL TEACHER IN BEIJING WOULD SAY TO HIS students, "You get what you get, and you don't get upset." This became a catchphrase in our family, and nine months after his diagnosis, Haydn recalled this statement lying in his hospital bed. Not once did he say, "Why me?" If anyone had even suggested such a question, he may well have replied, "Why not me?"

Many people seek to avoid tests and difficulties at all costs rather than accept. Haydn didn't. When he was twelve years old, we lived in Beijing, and Haydn tried out for a local soccer team called the Stormtroopers. He didn't make the team that first attempt, nor the second. At the start of the third season, Haydn showed up again equally as determined, and this time he made the squad. Throughout the seasons, he remained undeterred and resilient. Giving up was rarely an option for him, even as a young lad.

There is a Chinese proverb that says, "He who tastes the most bitter is the greatest of men."[1] In other words, only by withstanding the hardest of hardships can you hope to rise to greatness. After years of observation in China, I will generalize and say that this concept is a deeply ingrained aspect of life within Eastern societies. In contrast, Western societies seek to avoid pain and suffering wherever possible. The primary goal is to seek pleasure. At both the individual and societal levels, a pleasure-seeking life replaces a growth-seeking life. As a result, indulgence becomes the norm, and the inevitable hardships of life lead to disappointment and sometimes an inability to cope. How can one accept an uncomfortable twist in their life story if the conditioned response is to run from such discomfort?

When difficulties confront us, it is wise advice to confront them in return. You get what you get, you don't get upset, and you keep moving. Don't waste energy on avoidance. When climbing a mountain, this means putting one foot in front of the other. As long as we keep moving, we begin to see that our challenges are opportunities to strengthen ourselves, to build our inner resolve, to push beyond the discomfort. Everything in nature is in ceaseless movement, whether visible or not. If we aren't moving forward, by implication we are moving backward. The processes of integration and disintegration define the nature of growth and the growth of nature. Human beings are no exception. We also know there is no such thing as growth without pain. For the oak tree to be as strong as it is, the oak seed must break apart. When we look to nature, the metaphors and messages are boundless.

As we neared the end of Haydn's radiation treatments, we remained hopeful that in a few days he would be clear of cancer and given a clean bill of health. At this critical point, an ancient Chinese story tempered our anxiousness.

A long time ago in China there was a man whose total material possessions consisted of one horse. One day the horse disappeared, and the neighbor said, "O dear! That is such bad luck."

"Maybe yes, maybe no," replied the old man. The next day the horse returned with a herd of wild horses. To which the neighbor exclaimed, "Wow, that is such good luck!"

"Maybe yes, maybe no," replied the old man. A couple of days later the old man's son tried to get up on one of the horses but was thrown off and

broke his leg. When the neighbor heard of this accident he came around to the old man's place and said, "My friend, this is really bad luck!"

"Maybe yes, maybe no," replied the old man. That same evening the army sent their recruiters around to all the local villages to enlist every strong and able-bodied man in the region. With his broken leg, the old man's son did not get enlisted and stayed home to heal. On hearing the news, the neighbor exclaimed, "Now that is a stroke of good luck!"

"Maybe yes, maybe no," replied the old man.

We just never know.

Acceptance quickly topped the list of lessons learned during Haydn's journey. We found that acceptance provided a constancy and calm for what was a tempestuous, unknown, and arduous journey. Acceptance also captured the spirit with which Haydn took every step in climbing this mountain. Whatever his fate, he stood tall, faced forward, exhaled, and accepted all with grace.

It had been one year since that awful phone call—when Karyn and I learned that Haydn's MRI revealed a tumor. I recall a morning about that time when I sat and meditated, facing the lake and the hills that were Haydn's last view of this world. It occurred to me that acceptance was a strong tenet of this whirlwind, grief-stricken journey. That day, a group email arrived from one of my sisters. It began, "Acceptance is key. . . . " This was quickly followed by a note from my sister-in-law that said, "Not all things are acceptable!" Both were valid. And, of course, what my sister-in-law was saying serves as a critical counterpoint. Some things—many things—should straight up never have to be accepted.

Yet acceptance is critical to our coming to terms with our journeys. If we consciously choose to accept our circumstances and the totality of our lives, we can choose to not become helpless or upset in the face of challenge. Resilient people accept life's challenges and choose where and how they direct their attention, irrespective of their emotions. As it says in the Serenity Prayer:

God, grant me the serenity to accept the things I cannot change, courage to change the things I can, and wisdom to know the difference.

The quality of acceptance and bending to our fate requires a genuine openness and trust, whatever the outcome. From the beginning of this journey, whenever we went to doctors' appointments, Haydn's approach was, "Let's just go and listen, then consult and we will know." He didn't consult with a preconceived outcome. He made sure he conferred with all the right people, obtaining the best medical opinion we could find. And then he trusted in the result, whatever that might be.

Science has begun to investigate the true benefits of acceptance as an emotion-regulation strategy. In 2018, the *Journal of Personality and Social Psychology* published a study by Brett Q. Ford and fellow researchers Phoebe Lam, Oliver P. John, and Iris B. Mauss. They presented laboratory, diary, and longitudinal evidence that found:

Individuals differ in the degree to which they tend to habitually accept their emotions and thoughts without judging them—a process here referred to as habitual acceptance. Acceptance has been linked with greater psychological health, which . . . may be due to the role acceptance plays in negative emotional responses to stressors: acceptance helps keep individuals from reacting to—and thus exacerbating—their negative mental experiences. Over time, experiencing lower negative emotion should promote psychological health.[2]

As humans, we are really good at noticing threats, and negative emotions stick to us like Velcro. By comparison, positive emotions seem to slide off as if we were made of Teflon. These days, we exist within a flood of continual threats. Our threat response and stress levels remain dialed up, pushing our normal into an elevated state. This is not good for the immune system, nor for our mental and psychological health. Resilient people don't diminish the negative, but they have figured out how to tune into the positive. They find things to be grateful for, and they focus on those. In Haydn's journey, he focused on being at the lake house surrounded by nature rather than in the bustling cities of Toronto or New York. He focused on our being together as a family at home rather than in a solitary hospital room. As a family, we focused our reflections on nineteen years of an incredible and happy life rather than on the sadness of dying. For parents who lose a child in a sudden accident, they may feel grateful for being spared losing their child to a long, drawn-out disease. For the parent who watches their child navigate months or years of a debilitating disease, they may feel grateful for the time together, for the chance to prepare and say one's goodbyes. Is one more gentle than the other? Maybe yes, maybe no. What is clear is that the cup may be half empty, but it is also half full. And that is always worth celebrating.

A word of caution: the traditional view of categorizing emotions as either good or bad, positive or negative, can be overly simplistic and rigid. And rigidity in the face of complexity is not usually a successful strategy. We need emotional agility for resilience and thriving. Susan David, a Harvard Medical School psychologist, wrote the bestselling book *Emotional Agility* based on a concept the *Harvard Business Review* heralded as a Management Idea of the Year. Her 2017 TED Talk, "The Gift and Power of Emotional Courage," went viral with more than one million views during its first week, challenging a culture that prizes positivity over emotional truth and emotional agility. I leaned into her lessons and am entirely grateful for her insights.

In Western culture, which values uncompromising positivity, the key to well-being is to accept our emotions as they are, whatever they are, so we can process and progress. To improve our mental health and its resiliency, we do better to accept the fragility and difficulties of life rather than to pretend. Alas, we live in a world where shiny happy Instagram photos trick us into thinking that is, or should be, our normal life.

According to a 2020 study by the World Health Organization, depression is a leading cause of disability worldwide and is a major contributor to the overall global burden of disease—even more so than cancer or heart disease. According to Susan David, some 30% of the Western population either judge themselves for having so-called bad emotions—sadness, anger, grief—or actively push aside these feelings. We do this to ourselves as well as to others, most notably to the people we love, like our children, instead of helping them to see the entire range of emotions as inherently valuable. While sadness or anger may be deemed "negative" emotions, if we direct them against injustice or tyranny, can they not be the cause of positive change and progress? While happiness may be coined a "positive" emotion, if it is happiness at the expense of others, how positive is that? At the same time, happiness and joy do not exist without sadness and anger.

Emotions are not meant to be good or bad. Being positive is excellent, until it becomes a new form of moral correctness. When emotions are pushed aside, they only amplify, and the internal pain eventually comes out perhaps even more demonstratively. We lose our capacity to develop skills to deal with the world as it is rather than as we wish it to be or think it should be. Tough emotions are part of our contract with life. Discomfort is the price of admission to a meaningful existence and to personal growth. As was noted at the start of this chapter, there is no such thing as growth without pain. Clinical research shows that honest acceptance and processing of all our emotions is a key to thriving and authentic happiness.

Resilient people understand that suffering is part of life, part of every human existence. Understanding this stops us from feeling discriminated against when the tough times come. Instead of thinking "Why me?" the resilient person thinks "Why not me?" Such acceptance enables us to climb whatever mountain we have before us.

For sure, Haydn asked, "How are we going to do this?" but he never asked, "Why?"

> *The more difficulties one sees in the world the more perfect one becomes. The more you plough and dig the ground the more fertile it becomes. The more you cut the branches of a tree the higher and stronger it grows. The more you put the gold in the fire the purer it becomes. The more you sharpen the steel by grinding the better it cuts. Therefore, the more sorrows one sees the more perfect one becomes. . . . The more often the captain of a ship is in the tempest and difficult sailing the greater his knowledge becomes.*
>
> —'ABDU'L-BAHÁ, *Star of the West,* VOL. 14

For the Lord seeth not as man seeth; for man looketh on the outward appearance, but the Lord looketh on the heart.

—1 Samuel 16:7 (KJV)

O SON OF SPIRIT! I created thee rich, why dost thou bring thyself down to poverty? Noble I made thee, wherewith dost thou abase thyself? Out of the essence of knowledge I gave thee being, why seekest thou enlightenment from anyone beside Me? Out of the clay of love I molded thee, how dost thou busy thyself with another? Turn thy sight unto thyself, that thou mayest find Me standing within thee, mighty, powerful and self-subsisting.

—Bahá'u'lláh, *The Hidden Words*, Arabic no. 13

The philosopher is not influenced by praise or blame. He knows the truth and is not afraid, regardless of what happens to him in this world.

—Tao Te Ching, LXVII

3.

AUTHENTICITY

"I am who I am, and it is good enough."

THE CALCULATOR STORY WITH WHICH I BEGAN THIS BOOK HAS A
sequel. Having dealt with his forgotten calculator at the Wellington
exam with composure, Haydn relied on his mental arithmetic, a
product of the Chinese methodology of teaching math, to complete
the exam. But no matter how brilliant a person may be, completing
a high school math exam without the required calculator presents a
certain margin for error. Haydn didn't get an offer and was instead
wait-listed. He accepted this news with grace and gratitude. Three
weeks later, he received an email from the school: a place had become available, and it was his for the taking. Upon reading the email,
Haydn didn't dance or shout. He just beamed with a genuine, happy
smile. Consistently true to his form no matter the feat, and true to
the "maybe yes, maybe no" story, Haydn indeed embodied mindful
happiness or, to put it another way, *authenticity*.

When I asked Haydn's younger brother what he learned from
Haydn, Keyan didn't hesitate for a moment before saying, "Haydn
was authentic." When I asked him what he meant by this, he elabo-
rated, "Haydn knew who he was, and he didn't pretend to be someone else. He knew the path he was on."

Cisplatin was the workhorse of Haydn's initial twelve-week chemotherapy treatment. It is one of the powerful platinum drugs often

used in chemo, but it has a number of cascading side effects. For Haydn, one of those was hearing loss, combined with tinnitus, a continuous ringing in the ears. This started on day two of the first round and never left, although it was more pronounced at some times than others. In the grand scheme of things, having an incessant and continuous ringing in one's ears may seem like a small price to pay for the potential benefit of a drug that often plays a major role in destroying cancer cells.

Haydn didn't make a big deal of his tinnitus, and he reserved his time with his doctors to address more pressing issues. This must have taken a considerable level of strength. Haydn naturally did what athletes are taught to do when competing: tune out everything else and focus on the finish line. Run your own race.

"I am what I am, and it is good enough" is an affirmation used in courses by the Life Training Institute. It is a simple and useful reminder to stay true to oneself, which is a lot easier when we stop comparing ourselves to others. If we're running a race scanning our peripherals, we quickly become distracted, our forward focus reduces, and suddenly we're off pace, perhaps even falling behind. Yet when we stay sharp and in our own lane, we pace according to our own body and fully own the experience as that which we are naturally designed to achieve.

Unfortunately, many of our educational systems and much parenting are based upon encouraging competition rather than cooperation.[1] In terms of our daily lives, if this attitude of side-eyeing others as a means of determining one's own position is nurtured in day cares and kindergartens, of course children grow up believing that there is only one "winner," one person at the top of the class, one captain of the team, one gold medalist, one success story. For most of the class—everyone except the one who "wins"—the message of such a comparative and competitive model is the inevitable conclusion that the rest of us are not quite good enough.

For the most sensitive of us, this one-winner concept may translate to a simple message of failure and the beginning of a lifetime of frustration, low self-esteem, lack of fulfilment, completely unnecessary unhappiness, and repeated attempts to become something other than who we really are to get ahead. I believe the Western world is experiencing a crisis of culture, in which the majority of us are taught and encouraged by systems of divisive and partisan politics to see our world in polarizing terms: countries are developed or undeveloped, people and ideas are right or wrong, good or bad, religious or irreligious, "with us" or "against us." In such context, we are fed an equally polarized and polarizing picture of health that is binary, where some of us live in the kingdom of the healthy and others in the kingdom of the sick,[2] where we are either well or unwell, whole or broken, balanced or imbalanced.

It is a myth that there is some perfect state of wellness to be achieved and a double myth that such a state will bring us happiness. Such a myth perpetuates living constantly dissatisfied, feeling the need to become a different person. Such discontent is increasingly recognized as a source of modern illness, both mental and physical. The binary framework is a mental construct that may be useful in the production line of a factory making widgets, but it is woefully dangerous as a framework for understanding human wellness and building communities.

> *Each side hopes the conflict system will produce the winner who can protect them from the evil on the other side. The conflict system produces the friend and the enemy, orchestrates the contest, and fuels itself through the energies of the engaged. Some will cheer, others will cry, many will prepare for the next round of battle. The division will deepen. Should we place our faith in this conflict system?*
> —DAVID A. PALMER, UNIVERSITY OF HONG KONG

Research published in *Scientific American* by Jennifer Beer, a professor of psychology at the University of Texas, Austin, demonstrates a fascinating conflict or paradox between *being* authentic and *feeling* authentic.

Beer notes, "Authentic people behave in line with their unique values and qualities even if those idiosyncrasies may conflict with social conventions or other external influences. For example, introverted people are being authentic when they are quiet at a dinner party even if social convention dictates that guests should generate conversation."[3] The distinctive twist, however, is that "a number of studies have shown that people's feelings of authenticity are often shaped by something other than their loyalty to their unique qualities. Paradoxically, feelings of authenticity seem to be related to a kind of social conformity." Specifically, she notes that such conformity is usually applied to a particular set of socially approved qualities, such as being extroverted, emotionally stable, conscientious, intellectual, and agreeable. Beer offers an illustrative example:

> So, when it comes time to actually make a judgment about our own authenticity, we may use criteria that are closer to how we judge the authenticity of an object such as food. A passion fruit tiramisu may be unique, but the authenticity of tiramisu is judged by its conformity to a conventional recipe. Similarly, it appears that the more we conform to social conventions about how a person should act, the more authentic we feel.[4]

Authenticity is subtle and nuanced. When I think of Haydn's authenticity, I see a young man who was comfortable in his own skin and, beyond that, in his being. A word that comes to mind is *natural,* rather than forced or artificially compliant. His smile, his words, his actions, were genuine, usually understated rather than dramatized for effect. Consequently, he oftentimes had a dramatic impact on those around him, not because he tried for that but simply because of the power of his authenticity.

Haydn was brilliant at integrating, at staying himself while managing the input of the world around him. He would see situations, whether in the intimacy of our family life, in his own life, or at the scale of the human family, and he would be quick to connect the dots. It was like a great puzzle, and he had an uncanny ability to see what went where and how. It's no wonder he loved puzzles and playing games, especially games of strategy. Ironically, one such game we bought before COVID-19 tilted the world was the cooperative board game *Pandemic*. When playing *Pandemic,* Haydn took to it so much more naturally than the rest of us, and we would often find ourselves seeking his suggestions regarding strategy and the next best move.

Haydn taught me that there is profound beauty in seeking solutions through mutual agreement or reconciliation. He believed that the spark of truth can come from the clash of differing opinions, so we should embrace such diversity. What he avoided, however, was the adversarial approach to differences of opinion, where we see those who don't agree with us as our enemies and where we are always ready for battle.

Whether among family members or among friends, Haydn was the master reconciler. I believe this was mostly because he was so authentic and true to himself. Standing on firm ground makes it easier to give others a hand when they are slipping. It rarely took more than thirty minutes with Haydn to reach a resolution for the most intractable argument. He was a great listener to all sides without the veil of bias. He actively avoided judging others and was a natural peacemaker. Because he listened to all sides and then found ways to reconcile, he became something of our family's resident therapist—not an easy task with six unique personalities! On a few occasions, when siblings might be at odds with each other, Haydn would call them into his bedroom, close the door, and have a chat. The door would open in due order with a peace treaty in place. On a few occasions, when Haydn saw that Karyn and I were struggling, he called us into his bedroom, closed the door, and initiated a consultation to help us see and respect each other's point of view. Haydn didn't take sides but simply helped validate differing views, thereby helping us do the same.

We likely all aspire to stand on firmer ground, lending a hand to pull up others from whatever their quicksand may be. While Haydn was ever one to lend that hand, the uncertainties and regular setbacks of his journey through cancer turned the tables. His sense of self was surely challenged by the barrage of tests and trials, being the one lying helpless in a hospital bed, and eventually facing his own demise. He was fortunate that there were family and friends who rallied to his side lending whichever hand was needed. One friend, Camille, could always make Haydn—actually anyone—laugh. Camille lit up the room, perhaps because she was so true to herself. She had her own share of life challenges and was remarkably in tune with the nuances and strains of our every day. She didn't attempt to wear a costume of who she thought she should be during our storm, what she should or shouldn't say or do. To this day, it remains a mystery to me how Camille visited Haydn in Toronto, New York, and Ottawa, while convincing her professors in the UK that she was managing classes there.

Haydn didn't try to change his personality to become like anyone else, whether they were at the top of the class, with a more successful team, or even in better health. Haydn had a strong sense of self and was true to his path. Like bamboo, his strength derived from his flexibility, an uncanny ability to bend with the wind. He was not rigid or inflexible. Perhaps one might say if there was any place for rigidity it was to be rigid in principle but flexible in detail. He lived a life of coherence rather than juggling several lives of mutual exclusivity, all competing with one another for time and energy. He saw oneness and mutuality more naturally than he saw otherness.

> *We are caught in an inescapable network of mutuality, tied in a single garment of destiny.*
>
> —MARTIN LUTHER KING JR.,
> "LETTER FROM BIRMINGHAM JAIL," APRIL 16, 1963

As we each seek to find ourselves, define ourselves and our course, fight our own battles, realize our unique human potential, and share what we've learned, life becomes a call for authenticity, for being exactly who we are and realizing that we are each a unique creation of God. And, since God doesn't goof, we should have the courtesy to stop accusing Him of getting it wrong when it comes to others. One of the most grievous and revolting of all human errors is to judge another human being, rather than their actions. This also applies when the so-and-so happens to be ourselves. We must stop beating ourselves up. There is enough inherited carnage, pain, and suffering for the scars to likely take decades, if not centuries, to heal. Surely it makes more sense to nourish our lives with the affirmation that we are who we are and that we are perfectly designed for the life we are intended to lead. After all, are we not all working with God-created, God-directed, God-assisted raw material? Is that not good enough? To own such intrinsic confidence in who we each are, born not of ourselves but of our divine essence, makes an essential beginning for our ascent.

One of the most astonishing cancer stories is *The Journey,* a personal account by Brandon Bays. I read this book several years ago and found it to be so brutally honest and inspiring that at the time I bought ten copies to give friends. Diagnosed with a basketball-sized tumor in her uterus, Brandon Bays chose not to go the route of drugs and surgery but to embark on a path of natural healing and reconciliation. She describes that process in the most practical and accessible way, but it is essentially a spiritual process that accesses the healing power of the soul. Six and a half weeks after diagnosis, Brandon Bays was tumor-free and has been teaching her Journeywork process for more than twenty years.

> *This is the story of the journey home, and the soul's incessant call for us to recognize the greatness inside ourselves. . . . You are that which you are seeking.*
>
> —BRANDON BAYS, *The Journey*

At the heart of Bays' process is untangling whatever blocks us from coming home to the divine reality that is the essence of who each of us really is. That coming home is a profound experience involving reconciliation, forgiveness, understanding, the clearing of old "cell memories," and both spiritual and physical healing. When we were in Toronto, we reached out to a local Journey practitioner, who held a couple of sessions with Haydn. When I accompanied the practitioner back to his car after the first session, he turned to me and said, "Haydn is a remarkable young man. He is so wholesome."

Given such an observation, it was a mystery how or why he ended up with cancer. For the time being, the medical profession would say that it was just "bad luck," especially given that Haydn was in all other respects very fit, healthy, whole, and highly unlikely to be so afflicted. But life is much more mysterious than most of us, in our managerial complacency, usually accept and appreciate. These lessons from Haydn hopefully unfold some of that mystery and help us all to become more accepting and appreciative. There is goodness right in front of us. And even closer than that.

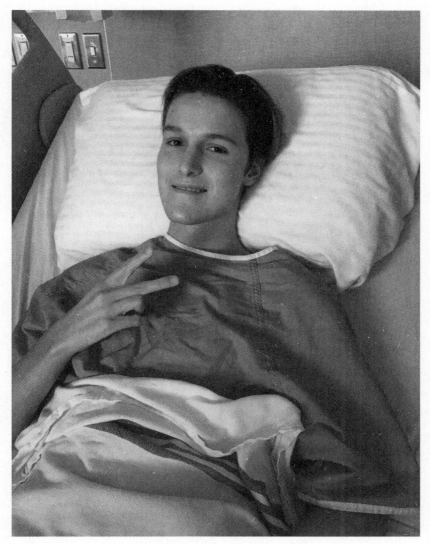

Haydn in hospital, Toronto; September 2019. *Photo courtesy of Karyn Robarts.*

If a man has ten good qualities and one bad one, to look at the ten and forget the one; and if a man has ten bad qualities and one good one, to look at the one and forget the ten.

—'ABDU'L-BAHÁ, *Bahá'u'lláh and the New Era*

The light shineth in darkness and the darkness comprehendeth it not.

—JOHN 14:1 (KJV)

Man's nature is naturally good just as water naturally flows downward. There is no man without this good nature; neither is there water that does not flow downward. Now you can strike water and cause it to splash upward over your forehead, and by damming and leading it, you can force it uphill. Is this the nature of water? It is the forced circumstance that makes it do so. Man can be made to do evil, for his nature can be treated in the same way.

—BOOK OF MENCIUS, 6A:2

4.

POSITIVITY

"Cause health!"

━━━━━━━━━━━━━━━

SOME MONTHS AFTER HAYDN PASSED AWAY, ONE OF HIS FRIENDS, Amelia, shared with us this exchange she had with him on WhatsApp, after he had been told by his doctors that there was no cure:

> *Amelia: You know, I try not to be sad because of the example you set for everyone. Because it feels kinda selfish for me to be sad.*
> *Haydn: Don't be, the next world is said repeatedly to be much better than here. And if our purpose in this life is to prepare for that one it should be approached with joy and happiness.*

At risk of being overly simplistic, we spend our lives drawn in to so much that is negative instead of drawn up by so much that is positive. For many reasons that have been well documented during the past twenty years, the significant bias of psychology and the social sciences in the twentieth century leans toward the negative side of the human experience. According to an article in the January 2000 issue of *American Psychologist* that effectively launched the field of positive psychology, social sciences, including psychology, have led us to believe that negative traits are authentic and that positive qualities—such as hope, wisdom, creativity, courage, spirituality, responsibility, and perseverance—are derivative or inauthentic. This is a phenomenon that has significant implications on education, politics, health care, and the media. The ever-shortening but ever-present news cycle is predominantly focused on the negative—the conflicts, dangers, injustices, intrigues, short-term horrors, and long-term potentials for even worse to come. To remain focused on the negative for any extended period without respite takes a terrible toll on our physical, emotional, and spiritual life, individually and collectively.

Prominent scholars, including Martin Seligman and Mihaly Csikszentmihalyi, argue that because negative emotions signal danger, they are more urgent and therefore often overpower positive emotions. Positive experiences, on the other hand, do not demand the same level of vigilance or alarm. They pass, most of the time, without any effort. Hence, the bias in psychology toward the negative may naturally reflect the value differences in the survival of negative versus positive emotions.

In 2005, Seligman and colleagues conducted a scientific experiment in which they asked half of the participants to think of three positive things that had happened to them each day. What they found was that those participants had higher levels of happiness, higher levels of gratitude, and less depression and stress over the course of the six-month study. How may we give ourselves encouragement—even permission—to accept the good that is usually right in front of us, even in the most miserable circumstances? In times of difficulty, including sickness, to be able to switch one's focus to also include the good has been shown by science to be a powerful strategy.

To further illustrate this, I offer a personal favorite and familiar story retold in several cultures. A grandfather is talking with his grandson, and he says there are two wolves inside of us that are always at war with each other. One of them is a good wolf, which represents things like kindness, bravery, and love. The other is a bad wolf, which represents things like greed, hatred, and fear. The grandson stops and thinks about it for a second. Then he looks up at his grandfather and says, "Grandfather, which one wins?" The grandfather quietly replies, "The one you feed."

In terms of human emotions, the warmth of love can entirely dispel the coldness of no-love. A thought of peace can dispel a thought of war. The same is true of hope dispelling hopelessness or happiness dispelling sadness. The power of presence eliminates the void of absence. The light of one small candle dispels the darkness of an entire room. I refer you to one of the scripture selections at the beginning of this chapter: "The light shineth in darkness and the darkness comprehendeth it not." In Buddhism, the word *avidya*, ignorance, means literally "the lack of light." *Vidya*, understanding, is made of light. In this manner, we can understand that an on-purpose, positive-centric approach can overcome the toxins of a negative lens and give way to an improved state of wellness.

—m—

Before World War II, the field of psychology had three clear missions: curing mental illness, making life more productive and fulfilling, and identifying and nurturing high talent. After, the focus turned almost exclusively toward understanding and treating mental illness. This focus had its benefits, as several "incurable" disorders were scientifically researched, and treatments to cure or relieve the symptoms were found. Psychologists came to understand how people survive and endure adversity, challenges, and trauma. The role of the practitioner focused on repairing damaged childhoods, damaged habits, or damaged brains. By adopting a disease-centric model, psychologists made remarkable progress toward discovering how to battle psychological damage. However, psychology's other missions, to promote productive, meaningful lives and nurture talent, became very secondary.

Conversely, positive psychology pointed to gaps in our knowledge about the potential for psychology to aid creativity, hope, and human flourishing. According to Seligman and Csikszentmihalyi's work:

Psychology has, since World War II, become a science largely of healing. It concentrates on repairing damage within a disease model of human functioning. This almost exclusive attention to pathology neglects the fulfilled individual and the thriving community. The aim of positive psychology is to begin to catalyze a change in the focus of psychology from preoccupation with repairing the worst things in life to also building positive qualities.

Psychology is not just the study of pathology, weakness and damage, it's also the study of strength and virtue. Treatment is not just fixing what is broken; it is nurturing what is best. Psychology is not just a branch of medicine concerned with illness or health; it is much larger. It is about work, education, insight, love, growth and play. And in this quest for what is best, positive psychology does not rely on wishful thinking, faith, self-deception, fads or hand-waving; it tries to adapt what is best in the scientific method to the unique problems that human behavior presents to those who wish to understand it in all its complexity.[1]

If we further extrapolate from these notions of positive psychology, we find a beautiful yet mostly unfamiliar method that exemplifies this positivity within the scope of health care. It's called the *saluto-genic* approach. The word comes from the Latin *salus*, meaning health, and the Greek *genesis*, meaning origin or creation. The term was coined in 1979 by the medical sociologist Aaron Antonovsky in his book *Health, Stress, and Coping*.

Antonovsky theorized that the way people view their lives has a direct physical influence, whether positive or negative, on their health. In 1971, Antonovsky presented the results of an epidemiological study in which he had interviewed a group of Israeli women who had been in concentration camps during the Holocaust. Despite the unthinkable suffering they went through, some of the women managed to stay in good health while others didn't. Trying to find an explanation for these differences motivated Antonovsky's development of the salutogenic theory. He based his theory on two core concepts: the *sense of coherence and the general resistance resources* (comprising biological, material, and psychosocial factors for people to perceive life as understandable, structured, and consistent). He explained health as a relative continuum and essentially found that an individual's sense of coherence explains why a person in stressful situations can stay well and, in some cases, even improve their health.

Although there are signs that the tide is slowly shifting, the focus of Western medicine is treatment rather than care or prevention. Although he may not use the term *salutogenic* in his book *Being Mortal*, Atul Gawande includes North American and Indian examples to make a powerful critique of how modern industrialized health care has made care of the elderly into a medical issue, of treating whatever ailments and frailties our elderly may have as a matter for doctors and hospitals to fix. This is a scenario doomed to failure and frustration, not to mention expense, as dying is eventually not fixable. Whether we are dealing with the elderly or a nineteen-year-old with a terminal disease, treatment has its limits whereas care is potentially limitless and always rewarding. The salutogenic approach is not just about promoting healthy, active poster people—rather it is the positive nurturing of health and caring for all of us, even if we are dying.

A well-respected medical doctor recently told me that his cutting-edge clinic is more like a high-tech company than a traditional hospital. He offered another comparison that was even more telling, saying that diseases in the body need to be diagnosed as early as possible—with which I wholeheartedly agree—and that the work of his clinic is to seek out those "terrorists lying in wait in the human body" and "take them out" with targeted precision and the best medical technology. This stereotypically represents the pathogenic approach to health: focusing on disease and then, as effectively as possible, "taking it out."

Sadly, the ominous reality of "taking out" a terrorist is not the same as "taking out" terrorism. When one destroys a malignant tumor in the body, or clears out a blocked artery, or removes a diseased organ, how do we know we are not just buying time until the next uprising in our body from any number of factors? To create health, we also need to find and heal the cause of terrorism in our bodies.

—◦◦◦—

Lessons in longevity and good health are out there. With Antonovsky's study in mind, perhaps the best hospitals are no longer "hospitals" in the ways we expect. I've visited a number of healing centers where the therapeutic benefits of music, art, cooking, dancing, and gardening are applied alongside Western medicine. This represents a significant shift from a *pathogenic* approach to a *salutogenic* approach, where the goal is to actually *cause health* rather than just to *cure disease.*

During our time in Toronto, Haydn learned about a Toronto-based architectural firm that is well known for its pioneering work in salutogenic design, led by the first Canadian architect to attain a master's in neuroscience applied to architectural design (NAAD). Haydn felt a resonance with this philosophy, and he liked several of their projects, which are elegant expressions of salutogenic design principles. Haydn believed that we need to understand and design for health and happiness in all human spaces. Once done with his chemotherapy and radiation treatments, Haydn planned to take some time, perhaps a couple of months, to "chill" and recover his strength and then begin an architectural internship with this firm as a precursor to beginning his architecture studies in the autumn.

It is increasingly clear that to achieve health rather than just health care, we need a much greater focus on prevention rather than treatment. The attitudes of our current health care systems are equivalent to building a wooden house in the jungle and then later coming up with strategies to eradicate the termites that have inevitably started eating the wood. An alternative strategy would be to build a house that is termite resistant in the first place. Even out of wood, that is both possible and proven, in some of the most far-flung and humble societies.

According to a 2018 study, the World Health Organization deemed cancer as the second leading cause of death globally, after heart disease, leading to one in six deaths. Around one-third of deaths from cancer are due to the five top behavioral and dietary risks: high body mass index, tobacco use, alcohol use, low fruit and vegetable intake, and lack of physical activity. As Haydn had none of these risks, he clearly fell into the two-third statistic.

Adopting the house-building metaphor, we might say Haydn was consciously trying to build a house that was healthy and termite resistant. Alas, we clearly don't know everything yet about what it requires to be termite resistant, or how to move from being termite resistant to becoming termite proof, or whether that is possible.

It is well observed that in human behavior the most intriguing is not the average but the improbable. Among the books beside Haydn's bed was *Man's Search for Meaning*, the inspirational classic by Viktor E. Frankl, an Austrian Holocaust survivor, neurologist, psychiatrist, author, and founder of logotherapy—a meaning-centered school of psychotherapy. I don't know whether Haydn had read it or was planning to read it, or whether it was a source of strength. After his passing, I reread Frankl's classic account of his struggle to hold onto hope during his three years as a prisoner in Nazi concentration camps.

Of course, Haydn's journey through suffering had none of the unconscionable evil or the deliberate and horrific torture that Frankl describes. However, Haydn's suffering was the worst I have personally witnessed: physically having to deal with unbearable, breakthrough pain from lumbar nerve root encasement with tumor and then psychologically having to experience a terminal disease take away his life and his future prospects. I mention this only to recognize that Haydn's positive energy and resilience enabled him to face his own formidable mountain and pass through his intense suffering with almost otherworldly grace, even gratitude, for all that he did have. Another inspiring example, for all of us, of what a human can become.

base camp

For we are saved by hope: but hope that is seen is not hope: for what a man seeth, why doth he yet hope for? But if we hope for that we see not, then do we with patience wait for it.

—Romans 8:24–25 (KJV)

Hope has its shadow of fear, or it is no hope.

—The Yoga Sutras of Patanjali, 4.24

Wherefore, if a man have faith he must needs have hope; for without faith there cannot be any hope.

—The Book of Mormon, 15.7.42

5.

HOPE

"Where there's life, there's hope."

PROPPED UP IN HIS HOSPITAL BED IN NEW YORK, HAYDN HAD TWELVE medics in his room during morning rounds: the oncology and transplant teams, the endocrinology team, the palliative team, and the nutritionist. On this particular day, the topic of consultation was changing Haydn's meds to reduce his orthostatic hypotension, feeling dizzy or fainting whenever he tried to get up. I watched in awe as Haydn read the room, expressed himself with clarity and calm, and articulated how he felt as he answered questions. His message to the team was pointed: "I'm willing to do the work; I just need these drugs to do their work. Giving up is not an option. If I'm going to die, I want to die knowing that I did everything I could."

What could have given Haydn the capacity to remain as positive as he did? The next three chapters—"Hope," "Faith," and "Prayer"—may be reflections on the obvious if you are a seasoned mountaineer or a scientist, or a person whose faith comes from meditating on life's lessons, especially its tests and trials. In that case, we can connect again in chapter 8, "Nature." Meanwhile, we will briefly address some of the most important tools to have in our pack—or, better, in our hearts—as we ascend the mountains that life presents us.

You may notice that these chapters slightly deviate from the widely known New Testament verse: "And now these three remain: faith, hope and love. But the greatest of these is love." (1 Corinthians 13:13, NIV). There is no chapter in this book on love. That is deliberate, because love permeates every chapter, just as it seemed to permeate every breath Haydn took during his climb.

Sanskrit has ninety-six words for love while ancient Persian has eighty. Yet, among some indigenous languages, such as Arop, one of the hundreds of tribal languages in Papua New Guinea, there is no word for love. Instead, the Arop show feelings of love through their actions. Some experiences are so powerful and sacred that no words are adequate to convey their power or sacredness. To reduce the reality of love to the word *love* is to risk trivializing it. So, I have chosen to tell the story and let the story tell us about love.

On October 21, 2019, our update email to friends and family included this note from Haydn:

Dear friends and family,

Today I was admitted into hospital to start my final round of chemo . . . this is great news as it means I am five days away from hopefully being done with chemo for the rest of my life! My platelet count this morning was at 123 (an acceptable number to start chemo) which surprised us all considering three days ago it was at 15. I'm sure this is a result of all of the prayers and positive wishes that everyone has been sending our way and I am incredibly grateful. On another note, I am feeling pretty good and have quite a bit of energy, so here's to hoping that keeps up throughout chemo and into the final recovery period! We are meeting with the radiation oncologist on Wednesday, which is a milestone as it signifies the next step in this journey... radiation. I can't believe the day has come and I'm excited for it to keep moving forward and to begin full recovery once radiation is complete—a point which seems much closer and much more attainable now that we are into the final round of chemo!!!

Sending much love and many thanks for any and all prayers that have been said!

Haydn

One of my favorite TED talks, and one of the most popular, with more than forty million views, is "My Philosophy for a Happy Life" by Sam Berns, a seventeen-year-old with progeria, a rare and debilitating disease affecting some 350 children worldwide. Sam passed away about a month after giving that heart-warming and inspiring talk, so full of happiness and hope. His first lesson for the rest of us was to "Be okay with what you ultimately can't do, because there is so much you can do." This was Haydn's attitude too. Here were two teenagers with rare and life-threatening diseases who deliberately chose to be grateful for all that they had—whether family, friends, or just the blessing of being alive.

Stephen Hawking was the most recognizable scientist of our age and himself a sufferer of a rare and degenerative disease known as motor neurone disease, or ALS. He was told he would live for two or three years when he was first diagnosed at the age of twenty-one. He died aged seventy-six. In his words: "However bad life may seem, there is always something you can do and succeed at. Where there's life, there's hope."

One aspect of hope is that it is forward looking. That is not to say that we should forget the past or ignore the present but that with hope we put these into perspective. Hope allows us to look forward to the future, thus making the present purposeful. Hope allows the past to be a firm foundation for our journey onward, rather than an unattainable destination evoked by sentimentally looking backward.

As a mountaineer gazes from the mountain and takes in the unfolding vistas, whether of the landscape below or of the next peak that beckons from above, the increasing beauty, awe, and wonderment is often so palpable that it can bring one to tears. Faced with the awesome majesty and scale of mountains, one appreciates how small one is in the world, both in stature and in the blink of time. One is humbled and hope filled, at the same time, realizing how much one can still achieve. The beauty, awe, and wonderment generate hope. The "weightlessness" of life brings new perspective.

Indeed, Haydn's journey seemed to have its fair share of both hopefulness and hopelessness. After some distance, I believe these were really just different lessons in hope.

In 1986, Václav Havel, while still a dissident and before he became president of Czechoslovakia, was asked this question: "Do you see a grain of hope anywhere (in the 1980s)?" This is part of his answer:

> *The kind of hope I often think about (especially in situations that are particularly hopeless, such as prison) I understand above all as a state of mind, not a state of the world. Either we have hope within us, or we don't. . . . Hope is not prognostication. It is an orientation of the spirit, an orientation of the heart. It transcends the world that is immediately experienced, and is anchored somewhere beyond its horizons. . . . I feel that its deepest roots are in the transcendental, just as the roots of human responsibility are, though of course I can't—unlike Christians, for instance—say anything about the transcendental.*[1]

In his book *Disturbing the Peace*, Havel went further to say:

> *Hope, in this deep and powerful sense, is not the same as joy that things are going well, or willingness to invest in enterprises that are obviously headed for early success, but rather an ability to work for something because it is good, not just because it stands a chance to succeed. The more unpromising the situation in which we demonstrate hope, the deeper that hope is. Hope is not the same thing as optimism. It is not the conviction that something will turn out well, but the certainty that something makes sense, regardless of how it turns out. In short, I think that the deepest and most important form of hope, the only one that can keep us above water and urge us to good works, and the only true source of the breathtaking dimension of the human spirit and its efforts, is something we get, as it were, from "elsewhere." It is also this hope, above all, that gives us the strength to live and continually to try new things, even in conditions that seem as hopeless as ours do, here and now.*[2]

That last sentence should give us at least some hope. It is hope that pulls us forward and keeps us on the climbing path. At the same time, it is overly simplistic to say that hope is *only* forward looking, for hope stands on the shoulders of what we have already achieved, of history. Hope stands on the shoulders of the mountain, or mountains, already climbed, by us or by those gone before us. Hope is not the same as wishful thinking. It is founded on firm foundations, or else it is indeed just wishful thinking. What is the firmest foundation for hope? I believe it is faith.

I dare to say, in the spiritual reality of the climb, faith is the mountain itself, on which hope stands firm. Hence "faith" is the subject for the next chapter. To take that step between these two interrelated lessons, herewith a touching story of hope and its implicit relationship to faith. It is part of a letter we received from a friend in Beijing:

> *I used to be an emergency medical technician and worked in a hospital emergency room. One day I was riding in the back of an ambulance with a patient—a female child perhaps 2-years-old. She was badly burned with third-degree burns over much of her body. At first, she seemed in shock and I prayed for her in the back of that ambulance, sensing the great tragedy before my eyes. And suddenly I felt such love all around us as I cannot describe. The child looked into my eyes with such trust and peace as we held hands. She was not crying or even shedding a tear, but I could see that she was fully conscious and in no pain.*
>
> *This experience was a great gift to me because it gave me the certitude that every soul, even going through the worst ordeal, is under God's watchful care. Something transcendent elevates all our experiences, so my existential questions were erased . . . about how God can allow tragedies to happen.*
>
> *There is no tragedy that cannot be transcended. . . . And maybe there is no tragedy that will not be transcended, even without our participation and agreement. Grace is that powerful and God is that good. Our suffering is lessened the sooner we trust in Him.*

It seems that the greatest mystery is His residence in us, behind the veil. . . . And that all of our anthropomorphic metaphors are inadequate to express our relationship to Him. We call upon Him as if He is "out there" and some "Other," while it is through His Light within us that we live and move and have our being. Yet, both are true. He is the great Beyond in the center of our lives. We will never penetrate this mystery in the condition we are now. It is amazing that He lets us know this and still keeps its deepest truth hidden from us.

This was a powerful letter for me. It is the religious frame that enables us to have hope through faith, that forgiveness and God's mercy will wash away the most terrible of tragedies, like sending them down the river to the sea. Without this divine benevolence we end up living in a battlefield of scars.

There is a danger that belief in an All-Loving God, the Essence of Forgiveness and Mercy, Grace, and Love, may blind the believer to the harsh reality of cruelty and crime, depersonalizing real tragedies that do exist. In the end, I chose to apply the logic of divine benevolence because it does make my life easier to deal with. I also believe that humans with the humility and belief in something more than ourselves, and a belief in the goodness that comes as a reflection of the Source of all Good, are capable of creating a world civilization that will be more altruistic, more noble, and more spiritually uplifting than an atheist or agnostic democracy, which promotes the survival of the fittest and a society in which we are, in so many manifestations, slaves to the strong.

Hope is really the light that can redeem our aspirations. It enables us to be optimistic in the face of adversity and to fortify our will to live fully. It is hope that enables us to fall and try again, rather than to give up. And every time we persevere with hope, we gradually build up our confidence and our faith. While faith may be the mountain, the firmest footing is hope. It is hope that in turn reinforces faith by giving us the confidence to trust in it and keep moving forward.

The Paralympics is an awesome arena of athletes who embody the powerful return on the essentials of hope. Lia Coryell, a two-time Paralympic archer, often questioned whether life with a debilitating disease was worth living. Coryell has progressive multiple sclerosis, a chronic, incurable disease that affects the central nervous system. When she relapsed seven years ago, landing in a wheelchair, doctors advised her to halt occupational and physical therapy, placed her in grief counselling, and urged her to settle her affairs. Tomorrow, they said, would never be better than today.

Since then, she has downhill-skied in Colorado, learned to play sled hockey, has taken flying lessons in a Cessna, and competed in the 2017 and 2021 Paralympics. Quoted in the official online news of the Tokyo Paralympics, Coryell proudly proclaimed, "I'm not resilient. I'm rebellious. . . . People don't expect me to achieve. They don't expect me to succeed. And it blows their world away because they don't have hope."

The essence of faith is fewness of words and abundance of deeds. . . .

—Tablets of Bahá'u'lláh, Asl-i-Kullu'l-Khayr

Thus reason and revelation go hand in hand; they support one another, and lead man to one goal; to happiness and truth.

—Moses Mendelssohn, Jerusalem, vol. 2

What five things lead to distinction? Five faculties: faith, energy, mindfulness, immersion, and wisdom.

—Dīghanikāya: Long Discourses, XXXIV:5.7

6.

FAITH

"Conscious knowledge expressed in action."

HAYDN'S CLIMB WAS A HEROIC STORY OF FAITH IN ACTION. WE PLACED our faith in our shared hopes and beliefs and in the best medical care available to us at the time. Then we acted on this with complete trust and conviction. This was a faith in both religion and science. There was no conflict in any of our minds between, for example, prayers for healing and chemotherapy for healing. While one was essentially spiritual, the other was clearly physical. The human being is both spiritual and material, so it is not illogical to apply healing in all aspects, to heal the whole person.

We all have faith. Some aspects of faith may be science backed and "proven:" every time we walk, run, or jump, even out of an airplane, we demonstrate our faith in the force of gravity and the laws of physics—at least as we understand them today—that define how that force behaves. Some aspects of faith are based less upon science and more upon experience, whether our own or our inherited cultural experiences that gives us confidence that we are on firm ground. For example, when a mother gives birth for the first time, it is a deep source of faith that she is doing what billions of women, over millions of years, have done before her and that her body is naturally built for this beautiful feat.

Sometimes we may have faith in less tangible things that science as we know it cannot fully predict or explain, such as friendship, love, trust, kindness, generosity, humility, and many other spiritual realities of life as a human being. And, yes, sometimes our faith may be more of a "leap of faith," like leaping out of an airplane with a parachute. But every kind of faith requires its terra firma that we are willing to trust to support our choice. If we had no faith in anything, we would be paralyzed and incapable of action. Faith is essential not just for material progress but also for spiritual well-being. I have yet to meet anyone who really has no faith.

Often what someone means when they say they have no faith is that they don't believe in the unknowable, things like God and religion. But it is perfectly reasonable to believe in what is unknown or unknowable, even in science. In fact, the scientific journey often begins with the application of the scientific method to investigate the unknown or unknowable, to get closer to knowing.

—·—

Faith is the heart of religion. At the risk of oversimplifying the most complex and mysterious of human experiences, the purpose and spirit of religion is to bring reconciliation and create civilization. Sadly, our history books don't always tell the story like this, and of course, we can't deny the heinous crimes and oppression that have taken place in the name of religion. But to enlighten and civilize the individual as well as society is the originating purpose of religion. So whenever the original light of religion is obscured by artificial interpretations and dogmas, it becomes time for religion to be renewed. This, in a nutshell, is the history of religion, the world's greatest civilizing process, and the seed of each of its civilizations. Without faith, religion is emptied. It becomes an empty shell, a lifeless body.

When we are going through a difficult situation, having faith and giving praise to God may seem counterintuitive. Consider the Old Testament story of Job, who lost so much in one day, including all ten of his children and his entire worldly wealth. Falling to his knees,

Job patiently declared, "The Lord gave, and the Lord has taken away." Job's praise did not cancel the facts. In spite of them, he followed those words with, "Blessed be the name of the Lord." Job was not in denial; he simply made a declaration. God had been good to him in the past and he could trust Him in the present. He had blessed him in the best of times, and He would not abandon him in the worst. God was too wise to be mistaken and too loving to be unkind. So even when walking through the darkest valley in his life, Job blessed the name of his Lord. To Job, God was the constant in his life. Praising Him and calling Him continually to mind demonstrated his trust in God and invited Him to his side. When I observed Haydn's forbearance and his patience under such unimaginable trials, I felt deeply humbled. Perhaps Haydn helped me catch a glimpse of being in the presence of Job.

Before Haydn passed away, he wrote a letter to his younger brother, which he entrusted to Karyn. No one else knew that he had prepared such a thoughtful, precious gift to be handed to Keyan after his passing. How did Haydn know that it would become a lifeline for the youngest member of the family, who would plunge into an awful grief? How does someone at the age of nineteen write with such conviction about such an unknown as to what lies beyond death? How does one write about such exquisite beauty when one is going through such pain? How do we see paradise when we are going through hell? For me, this exemplifies faith. With kind permission from Keyan, here is the content of Haydn's last letter:

> *If you're reading this it means I've probably passed away . . . despite everyone's best efforts to keep me in good health.*
>
> *I want you to know that that's ok! We all gave it our best shot and, ultimately, whatever happens is as God wills it. Please don't feel sad on my behalf, for I am in a better place . . . a place where evil doesn't exist . . . a place of pure love and joy . . . of this I am certain!*
>
> *Picture a beautiful garden, with life flourishing everywhere, with streaming water and radiant light. The sound of laughter in the air.*

The smell of fresh flowers . . . This is an image I've been using to keep me happy in the last few days. Whenever you feel sad, or depressed, or confused, close your eyes, take a deep breath, hear the water, and imagine us in that setting, in a world where there are no troubles!

Alternatively, if you're ever feeling down or sad because of my passing, turn to God. Say some prayers. Remember, I will always be around you, watching over you, and so is God. It may not make sense why there is suffering in the world, and why things like this happen. . . . I often wondered the same thing, and never quite understood it until these past few weeks. Suffering brings us closer to God and can make us realize things that we had never understood before. I truly don't think I've ever felt as much deep joy and happiness as I have over the past few weeks. I've felt closer to God, closer to our family, and I've had hope for a better world . . . one that is united, joyous, beautiful, and flourishing! I may never have felt this if not for my cancer and coming so close to death. So even though it may seem like a terrible thing from the outside, it has also brought about many positives!

I hope you can also see this or come to understand it in time, and I hope you always remember the joyous memories we've had, whether traveling to Laos and Cambodia, or saying prayers together in that little room in Toronto!

I love you so much!
Haydn

The binary framework—where we are either right or wrong, well or unwell, balanced or imbalanced—is a rigid and overly simplistic framework that propagates dichotomies where they rarely exist, at least according to science and reason. One of the most disturbing of these dichotomies is that we must choose between religion and science, or between faith and reason, between the heart and the mind, in terms of where and how to find truth. This duality, sometimes even seen as perpetual opposition between the heart and the mind, is based on misleading *definitions* of both faith and reason.

'Abdu'l-Bahá defines faith as "First, conscious knowledge, and second, the practice of good deeds."[1] No longer does such a term designate an acceptance of that which cannot be proven. Chapter 5 ended with the metaphor of faith as the mountain, or rock, on which one can have hope. That is the opposite of faith as fanciful thinking, superstition, irrationality, and blindness to fact—all the antithesis of knowledge, and far from being firm footing for hope.

'Abdu'l-Bahá also describes reason as "the first faculty of man" in *The Promulgation for Universal Peace* and also notes, in *Paris Talks*, that reasoning power "singles man out from among created beings, and makes of him a creature apart." He weaves together these concepts in *Divine Philosophy*:

> *God has given us rational minds for this purpose, to penetrate all things, to find truth. If one renounce reason, what remains?*

When reason is reduced to a particular type of rationality that confines itself to the realm of the empirical, it excludes everything that cannot be calculated and claims to be free from assumptions. Extremism, or dogmatism, can find its way into science, just as it has found its way into religion. One extreme leads to materialism, and the other leads to superstition. Reason and faith are complementary human faculties that together make possible the understanding of one's reality; they are both tools that enable us to discern truth.

In investigating conscious knowledge, in chapter 2, I noted Haydn's approach to our many meetings with doctors was to "just go and listen, then consult and we will know." He didn't go to appointments with preconceived outcomes. But he didn't go empty-handed either. He was on a quest for knowledge. He had an updated list of questions with him, usually typed in his phone notes. The doctors knew that they needed to allow enough time during their visits with

Haydn to go through his questions! Sometimes those questions were so thoughtful and well researched that the doctors also found them interesting and would stay awhile, just because it was enjoyable to have such meaningful conversation with this nineteen-year-old patient. And sometimes Haydn's questions didn't necessarily have concrete, explainable answers.

As we further our conscious knowledge in the spiritual realm, we begin to see that not everything taught by the world religions needs to be verified by science. On profound spiritual teachings about the nature of the soul, about life after death, about God . . . science has little to say. Similarly, spiritual teachings may be mute on the laws of physics or on how to perform triple bypass surgery. Broadly speaking, religious teachings tend to have more to say on spiritual reality—not only moral and ethical teachings but also how to nurture spiritual qualities or virtues such as love, kindness, compassion, forgiveness, mercy—whereas science tends to focus on material reality. The two are not at odds any more than the heart and the mind are at odds in a healthy psyche.

I find it interesting that so many geniuses on the frontiers of science may not have espoused a particular religion, but they were often very articulate and frank when it came to their awe of matters spiritual and their belief in some kind of divine power. Darwin said, "I have never been an atheist in the sense of denying the existence of a God." The same would be true of Isaac Newton, whose religious views were unconventional, but he was a theist nonetheless. Albert Einstein, who was raised as a Jew and later rejected the idea of a personal God, believed in a higher power and was not willing to call himself an atheist. Einstein's contemporary, Erwin Schrödinger, one of the fathers of quantum physics, was a devout student of Hinduism. There's a long tradition of leading scientists believing in religion and mysticism. Being a person of religion and science, even a hard-nosed research scientist at the forefront of theoretical physics, chemistry, or biology, is not a dichotomy to be resolved by mutual exclusivity. What is mutually exclusive is religious fundamentalism, such as the literal interpretation of the creation story or religious texts that are allegorical and whose power and beauty are in their metaphorical meaning. Scientists who are also religious believe, almost without exception, that much of scripture is allegorical in nature, that to investigate the nature of the universe is to fathom the work of God himself and to discover His creation in ever deeper glory. Such views don't contradict the tenets of scientific thought or principles; after all it was Galileo who said, "I do not feel obliged to believe that the same God who has endowed us with senses, reason, and intellect has intended us to forgo their use."

Neither the practice of faith nor the practice of reason means we won't have questions or doubts. Rather, we use our questions and doubts to deepen our understanding, through applying the scientific method and independently investigating truth for ourselves. I dare say that the ability to determine the most valuable questions to ask is a greatly underrated skill for education, for life, and especially for climbing difficult mountains.

Like anything living, faith grows, changes, gets tested through the vicissitudes of life, and also attracts confirmations from the spiritual realms. Haydn started his journey through cancer with a faith that may have been stronger than many other nineteen-year-olds', but does that even matter? What seems more relevant here is that Haydn's faith grew, deeper and wider, through his suffering and his journey through cancer. Haydn's letter to his younger brother is proof of Haydn's remarkable development as a human being during the previous nine months. This mountain companion got to know his young mountaineer well during his journey through cancer, and I can say, without equivocation, that the young man who started this journey—even though he was an outstanding scholar, athlete, and all-round human being—did not have the evident clarity and depth of faith as the author of the letter to Keyan.

I imagine that skeptics might read Haydn's letter and suggest that this is blind faith, for how can we ever know with such certainty? Especially about something as mysterious as the afterlife or God? It is beyond the scope of this book to adequately explain the development from faith to certitude. Perhaps a metaphor, which I heard from my own father, may suffice to intimate what I observed:

> *Imagine a traveler in the desert who looks into the distance and sees what appears to be the palm trees of an oasis. Fortunately for him, the oasis is also seen by his traveling companion, but because the day is hot and the traveling companion is wary, he questions whether the oasis may in fact be a mirage and not real. So they continue to walk on, until they see not only the palm trees but also the caravans and maybe signs of what might be people and camels. The traveling companion doesn't allow himself to believe quite yet, for the sun is scorching and it is surely possible that this oasis is being imagined, because he is thirsty and the sun's scorching heat may be playing with his mind. So they continue to walk on, eventually coming close enough to see with their own eyes that there are other travelers among the caravans, that there is movement with the sounds of chatter as persons replenish their water jugs from the wells and rest a while in the shade, refreshing themselves and their camels. At what point does the traveler know that the oasis is real? This is a journey from faith to certitude, when one actually drinks from the water of the well and tastes of its sweetness.*

One day, inspired by Haydn's extraordinary example, my sister-in-law turned to me and said, "Being inquisitive keeps you calm." She was a Montessori teacher, and Haydn was in many ways the quintessential Montessori student. Since kindergarten, Haydn exhibited the Montessori teacher's hope and dream for every child—independent investigation of truth. He was self-motivated to learn and had a genuine love for learning. By asking questions, and continually challenging one's current understanding, faith grows from fascination or superficial attraction to eventually become certitude or conscious knowledge.

In Book 7 of *The Republic,* Plato describes our experience of the material world as a shadow of the more real world. In his famous allegory of the cave, Plato wrote,

> *See human beings as though they were in an underground cave-like dwelling with its entrance, a long one, open to the light across the whole width of the cave. They are in it from childhood with their legs and necks in bonds so that they are fixed, seeing only in front of them, unable because of the bond to turn their head all the way around.*

As objects—whether people, animals, or any other object of matter—pass by the entrance of the cave, the outside light casts their shadows on the inside wall of the cave, which is watched by the cave dwellers who mistake the shadows for real, as they know nothing else. This shadow play naturally shapes and defines the entire worldview of the cave prisoners. Eventually, one of the prisoners leaves the cave and walks outside where he experiences the sunshine and a different "real" world. In this allegory, constructed in the form of one of Plato's dialogues, Socrates asks what the newly enlightened prisoner would think of his companions back in the cave. Also, if he returned back to the cave and told his companions what he had seen, they would probably think him crazy and reject him. The lesson from the allegory of the cave teaches that the imagined reality of what we think is "real"—the shadows—is in tension with the truth, or Truth, that is apparent to us only through our limited imaginations and experiences, and our limited minds.

In today's world, we might say that the dominant worldview is to believe in and pursue shadows based on acquiring money, education, fame, power, or "success," as these are ideas and social norms that permeate our systems of society. Unfortunately, this way of living is not leading us to increasing happiness or global harmony. So, how does one step out of the cave without simply moving into another cave or a different chamber of the same cave? For those people who have managed to get outside the cave, whether through their own efforts or through their encounters with others, it is not because they are any better than the fellow cave prisoners. It's simply because they made a conscious choice to question their reality and to independently investigate the truth for themselves, free from prejudice and the conditioning or consensus they have inherited from the family or the society into which they are born. To do this, we require the courage, and faith, to step outside of our comfort zone, to question our current understanding, to face fears and be willing to be authentic, even if that makes us different from the prevailing norms and expectations.

Haydn once said, "Keep asking questions. It's the only way we will learn, and it keeps people honest about what they are doing." Even at the very end of his journey, Haydn wanted to know what drug changes were being planned, and why, and what could be expected from those changes. Being inquisitive, while not being attached to the outcome, seemed to be Haydn's ice axe during his journey, his safety clutch. Being inquisitive, and accepting wherever the search takes us, is the nexus of reason and faith.

—∞—

When Haydn entered the Casa class of preschool at the age of three, his first teacher, Jessica, a Buddhist Montessori teacher, taught the children, among many things, to catch flies and gently take them outside rather than hurt them in any way. Six weeks before Haydn's passing, Karyn received a touching and tender email from Jessica, who had recently heard about Haydn's illness. This is an extract:

> *There is an intense sense in my heart that Haydn is at peace. When I light butter lamps during prayers for him, he always appears to me in my mind to be glowing and content. And I was wondering, why? I was contemplating this for a few days, and something occurred to me. Even from when he was a very, very young child as I knew him, Haydn*

seemed to have an infallible faith in God. He would speak with certainty and absolute faith when he would pray (and he had the cutest pronunciation as a young child when he would pray!). I remember it so distinctly. I might even go so far as to say it is the single most memorable quality I recall of him. Faith is not easy. One could say it is one of the most difficult spiritual qualities to obtain. And yet, when I think of Haydn, I think "faith."

It is beyond the scope of this book to adequately address what little we know about the mysterious relationship between faith and suffering. Perhaps future research will take us beyond anecdotal data and studies by the social sciences and shine the light of neuroscience or epigenetics on understanding how suffering affects resilience and other spiritual qualities. Meanwhile, here is a short but powerful reflection from Haydn on faith and suffering. A few weeks after we arrived in New York for Haydn's high-dose chemotherapy and stem-cell rescue, Haydn wrote a letter to a Bahá'í friend and mentor, whom he had been in touch with for a few years. Only after his passing, and in preparing for this book, did I get to know the contents of that letter, and I am honored to be able to share them here:

> *How do I stay firm in my faith? I keep getting these strong feelings of my belief and my faith, but it is pretty much only felt strongly while things seem bleak. . . . How do I maintain that solidarity and unshakable firmness of belief in the writings and the faith as a whole, and I feel great when I come back to this realization of the faith, yet when things seem easier, I find this realization harder to come by. . . . What does this mean and how can I try to keep this feeling around for longer or make more use of it?*

I was humbled to have associated with such an exceptionally truth-seeking, sincere soul, let alone that this was my son. It is clear to me that Haydn left this earthly plane in a state of heightened consciousness, and if he felt that his periods of intense experience were also those of increased depth of faith, then he departed this life on a remarkable high, a true Himalayan summit. I believe he has found his answers now and much more besides.

Haydn with his younger brother Keyan, New York; January 2020. *Photo courtesy of Pan Shiyi.*

And the LORD said unto him, I have heard thy prayer and thy supplication, that thou hast made before me: I have hallowed this house, which thou hast built, to put my name there forever; and mine eyes and mine heart shall be there perpetually.

—1 KINGS 9:3 (KJV)

Even if you do not reach His Essence, yet His remembrance has numerous effects upon you. You actualize tremendous benefits by invoking Him.

—JALÂL UD DÎN RUMI, *The Sufi Path of Love*

The wisdom of prayer is this: That it causeth a connection between the servant and the True One. . . . The greatest happiness for a lover is to converse with his beloved, and the greatest gift for a seeker is to become familiar with the object of his longing.

—'ABDU'L-BAHÁ, *Bahá'í World Faith*, 64.1

7.

PRAYER

*"One hour's reflection is preferable to
seventy years of pious worship."*

SINCE CHILDHOOD, HAYDN HAD A NATURAL LOVE FOR PRAYER. HE
memorized several prayers, some of them quite substantial. This was
particularly useful during his battle with cancer, when he was sometimes so weak that all he could manage was to close his eyes and find
solace and strength in conversing with his soul. One night, before
his fourth bout of five consecutive days of chemo, Haydn called me
to his bedside and asked if I would say a particular prayer. It was 3:00
a.m. as I began to recite this rather long prayer from memory. Just
beyond halfway through, I lost my way. Without missing a beat,
Haydn gently took over, intoning the verses that his tired father had
forgotten.

What happens when one places an iron rod into a fire? The metal rod, once gray and hard, cold and rigid, takes on the qualities of
the fire. It becomes orange and soft, hot and pliable. It begins to
glow and becomes radiant. What happens when one places an ordi-
nary human being into a state of being consciously present to the
divine? Our animal desires, material needs and wants, natural selfishness and ego begin to burn away and take on divine qualities of
kindness, compassion, forgiveness, and love. Selfishness burns away
and opens the way to selflessness. We become more radiant beings.

Prayer is the process of consciously placing ourselves into such a state. We might call it communion with our soul, or conversation with God, or connecting to the creative life force that sustains and energizes every atom, every molecule, every thing of beauty, every act of love and service, every smile, every law of science. Prayer is the most direct expression of faith that all these are real and have power to transform.

Haydn and I both grew up believing that prayer was the most powerful force in the universe. We also grew up well aware that for prayer to have such power it must "rise above words and letters and transcend the murmur of syllables and sounds," as described in a prayer by 'Abdu'l-Bahá. Such a prayer is really a condition or state of being, like that iron rod being placed in the fire. One can achieve a state of reverence and prayer through the recital of sacred verses and beautiful prayers, yet also through painting a beautiful painting, composing an uplifting piece of music, or working in the spirit of service. Simply put, prayers can take many forms and are not restricted to being taught in classrooms or religious services. One's daily life can be one's most effective prayer. And one type of prayer is not exclusive of other modes of prayer. More important than the form of prayer is the spirit in which one prays. In one of the hadiths, the traditions of Islam, it is said, "One hour's reflection is preferable to seventy years of pious worship."

In our home, when Tallis and Haydn were about five and three, we realized that wherever we placed emphasis, our children would likely do the same. So we converted the children's little playroom into a room for prayer and meditation. It was the most serene room in the house, with very few furnishings or distractions. We would sit on a beautiful Indian rug and say, or sing, morning and evening prayers. Haydn usually sang, louder than the rest of us, perhaps because he could more confidently carry a tune. Afterward, one of the children would gently hit the Tibetan brass singing bowl that we bought in a local antiques market. We would then sit in stillness until the sound entirely disappeared.

These words, from a talk by 'Abdu'l-Bahá in Paris (1911), were put to a song that was one of Haydn's favorites. It seems apt to share here in the context of reflecting on prayer:

> *Therefore, strive that your actions day by day may be beautiful prayers. Turn towards God, and seek always to do that which is right and noble. Enrich the poor, raise the fallen, comfort the sorrowful, bring healing to the sick, reassure the fearful, rescue the oppressed, bring hope to the hopeless, shelter the destitute!*

During Haydn's journey, there were many times—perhaps too many to count—when things didn't go the way I expected or the way I wanted. Thankfully, Haydn was more acquiescent, although there were a small handful of occasions when he, too, was stretched to his limit. On the one hand, the curative journey through cancer treatments was tough and unpredictable, so we were braced for the unknown. Guided by skilled doctors and nurses, Haydn was able to understand and deal with the many side effects of the treatments, including the tinnitus previously mentioned, the almost unbearable neuropathy in his hands, feet, and, at times, his entire legs, to mention some. On the other hand, there were multiple occasions when things went wrong that seemed to have little to do with the journey through cancer. Whether that was dealing with an extremely painful and persistent fissure for several months, or sharp and sometimes debilitating pelvic pains that also persisted on and off over several months, or unsuspected and undiagnosed chest pains that would sometimes make it hard to breathe. These added ailments seemed over and above what we anticipated or what the doctors could confidently explain. These were times when my heart literally ached to see my child experience such suffering, and I naturally reflected on the relationship between my will and the Will of God. How can one understand the Will of God? And how can one bring one's personal will into parallel with the Will of God? I believe that this is a key purpose of prayer.

In the fire, the iron rod gives up its inherent base qualities when subjected to the qualities of the fire. In prayer, we subjugate our will, our personal wishes and aspirations, to the greater presence of the Will of God. And in so doing, we are able to manifest the qualities of the Will of God in our lives. This happens at the deepest level of the soul, which is really the aspect of our being that is most effected by prayer. This alignment also manifests itself in the quality of our thoughts and the choice of our actions. This is not easy, especially when our personal will may be fixed on a clear target or outcome. It is not a compliment when we say that someone is stubborn or willful, because in our hearts we know that the insistent self, the force behind the willful individual, is inflexible, hard, and difficult to love. We all have some of that inflexibility and stubbornness, and at times that can be a useful quality to get us up those tougher slopes of the mountain climb. So we justify it, often at our own expense, especially in the long haul. There are ways to climb mountains without the inflexible, dogged determination that simply drives us up the steepest slopes at all costs. Just watch a mountain goat and see. People who pray, deliberately doing so in order to bring their personal will into harmony with the greater Will of God, become less like steamrollers and more like mountain goats in the way they manage mountains, or deal with the inevitable challenges of life.

We will come back to the Will of God and its relationship to nature later. Let us briefly reflect here on a metaphor from 'Abdu'l-Bahá, in explaining free will, which is surely one of the most precious gifts of being human, yet also our greatest test if it is not brought into alignment with the Will of God. In the book *Some Answered Questions*, 'Abdu'l-Bahá compares each individual to a steamship on the sea. "The motion does not arise from the ship itself but from the wind or steam." Our free will is akin to the rudder of the ship, for, "in whatever direction the rudder is turned, the power of the steam propels the ship in that direction. If the rudder of the ship is turned to the east, the ship moves eastward, and if it is directed to the west, the ship moves west." In this metaphor, one realizes that free will and predestination—that baffling subject that has perplexed philosophers and scholars of religion and science alike for centuries—are not mutually exclusive. Yes, we have free will, and this is a precious and sacred human gift. But that free will is subject to and relies upon a greater power to propel us forward, indeed to enable that free will to have purpose and direction. That is not to say that if the wind blows to the east, then ships can only sail eastward. A skillful sailor or captain of a ship can sail in the opposite direction to the prevailing wind if needed.

The message, as I have come to understand it, is that the ship can sail only if there is a wind or a force to power it along, and that the use of the rudder—that is free will in our case—requires each of us to accept and comply with that force. Prayer is a powerful tool to help bring about such alignment. In ways we can't dictate or even foresee, prayer enables us to live with purpose, powered by unseen forces we may not fully understand but which we can certainly feel, whether in the moment or in retrospect.

—⁂—

Surely it is not a coincidence that across the entire human family, scattered across the vastness of planet Earth, there is a consistent trait that all societies turn to prayer for those who have died. This phenomenon applies, irrespective of our cultures, religions, history, education or other labels that we so often use to define us, and divide us, as human. Surely this is one proof for the continuance of spiritual life beyond the veil of physical death, if that needs proof.

Prayer is conversation with God. But it is more than words. It is a spiritual attitude. I believe the power and effect of our prayers are conditional upon the love in our hearts, far more than the actual words we may utter or intone. In the scriptures of the world's faiths, prayer is described as the natural and inevitable expression of love: of the lover for the beloved. How could a lover resist to express such a love in whichever way one is drawn to do so? To pray requires faith that the beloved of our hearts is an all-loving, prayer-hearing, prayer-answering God, who assures us so, even if our prayers are not always answered in the ways we may hope. To me, prayer and love are equally mysterious, equally powerful, and very much related to each other. Prayer without love is at risk of being mechanical, just as love of God without prayer risks being frivolous. To scale any mountain, we can be neither purely mechanical nor frivolous. In the coming chapters, I hope you take courage from Haydn's climb to his summit and taste the sweetness of his humble but assured reliance on prayer in getting there.

While I believe in the power of prayer and have many personal experiences of remarkable confirmations that are hard to explain other than through that power, I confess that I do not understand prayer. How this works remains a mystery. There are a number of double-blind, randomized research studies, particularly in the context of health and healing, that have demonstrated that prayer does indeed have a demonstrable power. One pioneering study, conducted in 1998 by Mitchell Krucoff, evaluated the use of various noetic therapies, including prayer from a variety of religious practices, on 150 cardiology patients. Krucoff, a practicing cardiologist and professor of medicine at Duke University, found that those in the prayer group demonstrated between 50–100% reduction of adverse effects following angioplasty and cardiac catheterization compared to the control group without prayer. Studies around the globe, in different contexts, have yielded similar results. The work of Larry Dossey is particularly fascinating in this respect. Dossey wrote several books on the subject, such as *Healing Words: The Power of Prayer and the Practice of Medicine*, and delves into the role of intercessory prayer and distance healing. Conclusively, prayers for someone who is ill seem to be equally effective when said from the other side of the world or at their bedside. These are exciting discoveries, yet that doesn't make them any easier to understand.

When I pray, I often use the Bahá'í prayers, which to me are beautiful and poetic. During their lifetimes, the three central figures of the Bahá'í Faith—the Báb, Bahá'u'lláh, and 'Abdu'l-Bahá—revealed a number of prayers, whether for general use or for specific purposes such as health and healing, aid and assistance, protection, and family. These also include some particularly moving prayers for the departed.

In our regular update emails, there is not one that does not mention prayer. It was not deliberate; however, it is a reminder of how prayer was so integral to this journey. For me, saying or singing prayers together was a highlight of our days. Prayer lifted our spirits from the material challenges that were so obvious and so demanding of our time and energy. Prayer brought us joy and relief. It also connected our hearts to the many friends and family around the world who were praying for us. I also believe that it helped us accept with humility and awe that we were really not in control of the outcome of this climb. In a journey that had an ample share of hard edges—as one oncologist said to Haydn, "Yours has been a very rocky road!"—prayer brought a softness and tenderness that cushioned the knocks and lightened the load.

—ɷ—

If prayer describes what happens when we turn our souls toward God and commune with Him, then the reciprocal part of the communication is when we put ourselves in the receiving mode and receive His guidance. Meditation is that process. It is often described as synonymous with mindfulness, but for our purposes we will consider meditation as an essential practice to develop mindfulness. I have yet to meet a serious mountaineer who doesn't meditate, in some form or other, as a means of climbing mindfully.

There are many forms of meditation, and it is beyond the scope of this book to offer even a cursory summary, let alone to go into all of them. There are literally thousands of excellent courses on meditation available, whether in person or online, whether directly teaching meditation or, for example, examining the meditative practice through the scientific lens of evolutionary psychology or neuroscience. A number of acclaimed and sought-after academic courses are provided through top universities, including Harvard, Yale, Princeton, Rice, whether directly or through online portals such as *Coursera* or *Udemy*.

I wholeheartedly recommend *Full Catastrophe Living*, by Jon Kabat-Zinn, as the gold standard program on mindfulness, meditation, and healing. This highly readable classic about the healing power of mindfulness describes the mindfulness-based stress reduction (MBSR) program first implemented by Kabat-Zinn and his colleagues in 1979 through the Stress Reduction Clinic at the University of Massachusetts Medical Center in Worcester, Massachusetts. Since 1979, more than twenty-five thousand people have completed this evidence-based training. The results are so impressive that they necessitated a revised and updated edition of the program, twenty-five years after its initial launch.

—⁂—

When I reflect upon my own life and my attempts to meditate, one of the most profound and uplifting—indeed soul-nourishing—moments was when Karyn and I were with our two youngest, Haydn and Keyan. Together we were doing a walking meditation at a sacred Buddhist temple in Laos. This simple act of walking mindfully—being in present-moment-awareness with each step, treading with a sense of reverence on the humble ground beneath my feet, and breathing—brought me a memorable sense of calm and joy, and a simple lesson: meditation happens when it is not forced. As a cautionary endnote to this short reflection on meditation, I have found it useful not to be too attached to any particular form or practice of meditation. With meditation, one is really spending time in a spiritual condition, to nourish and guide the spirit. The form of meditation is entirely secondary to the spirit of meditation.

high camp

Nature is God's Will and is its expression in and through the contingent world.

—Bahá'u'lláh, Lawḥ-i-Ḥikmat (Tablet of Wisdom)

Know that Nature and Spirit are both without beginning [and] know [also] that all modifications and all qualities spring from Nature. Nature is said to be the source of the capacity of enjoying pleasures and pains. For Spirit, dwelling in nature enjoyeth the qualities born of Nature.

—Vyāsa, "The Mahabharata 6," 37.1

Nature that is not directed by the spirit is not true but degenerate nature.

—I Ching, 25.2

8.

NATURE

"Think of yourself as a river."

———————————

HAYDN LOVED WATER. HE LOVED THE SIGHT, SOUND, FEEL, TASTE, AND even the smell of water. Most especially, he loved the ocean, where he could enjoy long walks along its shore, surf its waves, dive into its depths, or just stand facing out to feel and taste the spray of sea-salted waves breaking against the rocks. Haydn's happiest holidays included the ocean, wherever that may have been.

When Haydn met with his palliative care doctor in Ottawa, he was asked whether he had anything that he would still like to do in whatever time remained before he graduated from this physical world. Haydn had only one request: could he make one last trip to the warmth and ocean of Sri Lanka? Although he didn't see his beloved ocean again, Haydn spent his last weeks by a lake in Quebec on the French-speaking side of the St. Lawrence River that roughly defines the provincial borders between Quebec and Ontario. When Haydn and his siblings were very young, we bought this simple two-bedroom cottage, no more than 650 square feet in all, and spent many happy summers there. Later, we demolished it and built a permanent home on the same plot, adding another bedroom and using natural materials—predominantly stone and wood—that celebrated the beauty of the environment and enhanced views of the forest, creek, and lake.

Our lake house became a sanctuary of serenity and beauty. During his final eight weeks there, Haydn moved between three rooms, starting off in the "white" bedroom, the calmest and furthest from the central hubbub of the living room and kitchen. The white room faces the woods at the back of the house and has a window at the foot of the bed that looks through the pine trees to the creek. It feels protected and embraced. The room has a second bed, where I slept so I could help Haydn with any needs, including administering his pain meds. When it was my turn to sit in the chair beside Haydn's bed and massage his legs, I marveled at this journey. In their nineteen years, those legs traveled many miles, played some respectable soccer, and spent ample hours in the gym. In the previous nine months they had became emaciated and weak, at times were sore and so tender from neuropathy caused by chemo that massage was out of the question. Once the neuropathy had subsided, Haydn appreciated our therapeutic and healing touch. Holding those feet in my hands felt like a gift beyond measure, a chance to bring some small comfort at the end of an arduous climb. It also gifted a moment to appreciate the imprint those feet had made on the world, even in a journey cut short.

From that chair, I could look out the window to the woods and admire the majesty of the tall trees. From March to May, I witnessed the scene change from a winter wonderland, with branches heavily laden with snow, to the leafy springtime of greens and yellows. Birds arrived, along with squirrels and chipmunks, and the creek hosted the activities of its native otters and beavers. As the days became a little longer, the sun thawed the frost and the ground sprouted its first growth of the season, which budded into spring flowers and displayed the beauty of seasons transitioning.

Being present to this awesome theater of nature in all its glorious details was a first for me. I wrote in one email update that I felt like I was in a David Attenborough film watching the birth of spring. As this happened slowly and gently, each day opened a new vista of nature's wonder, and I found it deeply affecting my thoughts and my prayers. Usually, I would pray with my eyes closed to reduce distraction as I communed with my soul. Here I began to enjoy praying with my eyes open, looking out of the window and drinking in the profound beauty of nature, being aware of, and present to, its life-giving energy and somehow visualizing that I was channeling that life force into the room and into Haydn's ailing body.

It is easy to talk about oneness, but the feeling of oneness is beyond the capacity of words. It is a mystic experience, a deep feeling that all things are connected to one another. Perhaps, in those moments, I experienced a taste of transcendence. I took comfort in my being a part of that connection. I could choose to become like a hollow reed and let this spiritual force flow through me to others. As humans we need to make a conscious choice to connect and align ourselves with this oneness that some may call God or, more precisely, the Will of God. When one brings this awareness into one's prayers, then prayer becomes a state of being rather than anything to do with words.

—⁊⁊—

Chapter 1 noted that the grand teacher that is Mother Nature can turn around even the most well-equipped and well-trained team with an unexpected storm. Haydn's cancer was one such storm, destroying his body from the inside. The onset of COVID-19, which started moving into New York at exactly the time that Haydn arrived for his treatments, was a parallel storm that began to shake up the body of our wider society. Interestingly, back in December 2019, when news of COVID-19 was just a whisper from China, Haydn was already concerned by its implications. He seemed to have a sense that this whisper would grow, with a gale-force wind behind it, and unleash havoc throughout the world.

Our relationship to the natural environment around us is perhaps the most critical issue of our time. This relationship is fundamental to the well-being of the planet and to our future as a species.

I remember Haydn saying that COVID-19 was far more than just a virus to be cured. In environmentalist Al Gore's book *Earth in the Balance*, Gore quotes this insightful passage from the Bahá'í writings:

> *We cannot segregate the human heart from the environment outside us and say that once one of these is reformed everything will be improved. Man is organic with the world. His inner life molds the environment and is itself deeply affected by it. The one acts upon the other and every abiding change in the life of man is the result of these mutual reactions.*[1]

—⁕—

Being in, around, and within nature is vital for our health and well-being. There is growing evidence that it also helps us to heal physically. In 1984, *Science* magazine published a study by R. S. Ulrich that examined the restorative effects of providing patients with a view of nature. Ulrich's research specifically observed the effects on pain and antianxiety medication use and recovery of patients who had undergone open cholecystectomy for gall bladder removal. The existing records of cholecystectomy patients in a two hundred–bed suburban hospital in Pennsylvania were examined. From their hospital beds, patients had either an unobstructed view of a small stand of trees or a brown brick wall. Other than the differing window views, the rooms were nearly identical in size, arrangement of beds, furniture, and other major physical characteristics.

The findings of Ulrich's study showed significant differences between the tree-view patients and brick-wall-view patients in terms of length of patient stay, use of pain medication, and nurses' notes. Patients with a view of trees were hospitalized shorter, an average stay of 7.96 days, compared to patients who had a view of the brick wall, an average of 8.7 days. The tree-view patients more frequently received weaker pain medications like aspirin or acetaminophen, while brick-wall-view patients needed stronger pain medications such as narcotics. Patients with the tree view had more positive notes, approximately one more per patient, which included statements such as "in good spirits" and "moving well." Patients with a brick-wall view had three times more negative nurses' notes, almost four more notes per patient with complaints such as "upset and crying" or "needs much encouragement." Ulrich's research concluded that natural views had therapeutic influences on hospital patients.

I wish that research like this was mandatory study in schools of architecture and for hospital administrators. Most emergency rooms and intensive care units I have visited have little or no natural light, let alone views of nature. I have yet to visit an operating room that has natural light, although I know a few do exist. The architectural firm I mentioned earlier designed the world's first underground radiation bunker to include natural light from skylights strategically positioned so that the radiation from the linear accelerators could not leak out of the bunkers. Often, when we accompanied Haydn to his radiation treatments in Toronto, I would think of how some natural light for the patients, and especially the staff working in this high-tech, state-of-the-art facility in the basement of Toronto's leading cancer hospital, would brighten their days, literally.

Each time Haydn was checking into a hospital, Karyn would inevitably ask if he might have a room with a view. Of course, we were fortunate to get a room of any kind, so this was not a conditional request, but it was always a tonic to the soul to walk into a room with a view, especially if it included water. In Toronto, we occasionally had views of Lake Ontario, even if just between buildings, and in New York, the Hassenfeld Children's Hospital is beside the East River. We were sometimes lucky, and always grateful, for these views. Unlike Ulrich, we didn't gather any scientific data to demonstrate any impact on Haydn's health, but anecdotally we noted the effect on Haydn when he walked into the inpatient room on the twelfth floor of Mt. Sinai hospital after thirty hours downstairs in the ER with no natural light. He simply couldn't stop smiling.

—⁂—

Nature is not only a powerful source of healing but also an extraordinarily powerful source of rich metaphors for living. A mountain stream is a beautiful and poetic reminder of the flow of life. Starting in tiny streams, life-giving water flows ever so gently. As water meanders down the mountain, delivering important organic material that supports life cycles, streams merge with other streams and become rivers. The ability to sustain life widens and stretches, as rivers make their way to the mighty ocean. The ocean is of course the most powerful metaphor of humility: it is the largest and most powerful body of water simply by being lower than all the rivers.

When Haydn was growing up, he heard this beautiful analogy of life as a river, from his much-loved "Uncle Alí."[2] It went something like this:

Each of us is like a river of life. As it happens, this river flows not through the desert, or through green meadows, but through a forest. Inevitably, as there are abundant trees in the forest, dead leaves fall into the river and are carried along by the running water. Sometimes there are also twigs that fall into the river and are carried along too. This dead debris is added to the river just like the difficulties and challenges that are added to our lives. They can be physical challenges, like ill health; psychological challenges, like developing loving and creative relationships or managing the demands of work and school; also spiritual challenges, like coping with deceit, injustice, or unkindness. These tests and difficulties can be overcome and be regarded as opportunities to strengthen and purify us. Where there is a forest, dead leaves will be present.

There are many things that, like the dead leaves, fall into our lives. This is not their fault, nor ours, but simply in the nature of rivers that flow through forests. Our negative thoughts can also be like these dead leaves or debris; they come to us and are normal and nothing to worry about. They cannot hurt us, so long as we let them move on downstream without getting stuck or blocking the flow of the water. We are not to blame or to feel guilty for having negative thoughts, unless we cling to them, nourish them, and act upon them. Only then can they potentially harm us or be destructive to society—for we can be sure that we are not the only river flowing through this forest. We are part of a network of waterways that is making its collective way through the forest, eventually to reach the sea. Perhaps the most important detachment is to let go of negative or destructive thoughts and let them flow through the forest without gathering and blocking the flow of the water that is our river.

As this river of life flows through the deepest part of the forest, dead branches fall into the river and may get stuck in the riverbed, accumulating and blocking leaves and other debris, and now make a dam. The dam may stop the flow entirely or may force the river to bifurcate and become separate streams, sometimes, but not always, joining up further on in their journey downstream. Instead of the river being a strong flow of water, the smaller streams can be rather weak, almost reduced to a trickle so that very little water is reaching its destination. In our lives this is like the depletion of our energy—physical, mental, or spiritual—so that less and less of our true potential is being fulfilled. What are those branches that caused this dam? They may include prejudice, pride, selfishness, suspicion, neglect of responsibility or obligations, to mention a few. What can we do about this blockage that has created our dam?

At this point in the story, Uncle Alí would smile and say, "Give it a kick!"

We need to apply the "kick" of firm resolution, faith, prayer, meditation, service, and obedience to the laws of the universe—we may call them God's laws—so that the water flows again. Stagnant water isn't good for us, or for those around us, or for the forest. It is the purity of the water of our lives that attracts others to us and allows us to spiritually nourish them.

Verily, I say, this phenomenon is the most mysterious of the signs of God amongst men, were they to ponder it in their hearts. . . . The world in which thou livest is different and apart from that which thou hast experienced in thy dream. This latter world hath neither beginning nor end.

—TABLETS OF BAHÁ'U'LLÁH, 12.19

And they said unto him, We have dreamed a dream, and there is no interpreter of it. And Joseph said unto them, Do not interpretations belong to God? tell me them, I pray you.

—GENESIS 40:8 (KJV)

Thou art he that has good dreams.
Thou art a mirror in which the universe is reflected.

—VYĀSA, THE MAHABHARATA 13, 17.2

9.

DREAMS

"Maps from the mountain."

IN THE TWO WEEKS BETWEEN DECEMBER 19 AND JANUARY 2, HAYDN recalled three very vivid dreams. In the first dream, he was being chased "by two Chinese Ninja attackers." Haydn used playing cards to defend himself, throwing these at his attackers, who eventually bowed in submission. In the second dream, Haydn was being pursued through the aisles of a massive Chinese supermarket and was pulling the goods off the shelves to save himself and stay ahead of his pursuer. In the third dream, Haydn was running from his younger brother, me, and the sniffer dog that was with us. This was a run for his life through the woods behind the old lake cottage. In this dream, Haydn found himself having plenty of energy, doing parkour and driving a getaway Jeep down a steep hill. It was a high-energy chase with high stakes. Yet this dream was at a time when Haydn was weak and nearing the end of five months of aggressive cancer treatments. Collectively, these dreams entailed Haydn being chased and running for his life.

In climbing mountains, especially at higher altitudes, it is common to experience vivid dreams, caused in some part by the combination of the thinning of the air and increased cycles of sleep. Anecdotally, it seems to me that at times of unusual stress and challenges in our lives, we may be more susceptible to stronger and clearer dreams. Whether we remember them or not is a separate issue.

In 1899, 'Abdu'l-Bahá said in the *Star of the West,* "There are three kinds of visions or dreams. First, those that arise from over-excited nerves, or disordered stomach, and are of no use what-soever. Second, when God sends a revelation to a soul that is not entirely pure from the world. To such ones He sends visions in symbols and signs, and these experiences need an interpreter. The third kind is when a soul who is severed from the world receives a revelation from God. In this station everything is clear and pure and needs no explanation."

Given that Haydn wasn't eating cheeseburgers late at night and knowing that neither he nor I would ever consider ourselves to be souls "severed from the world," I am only able to share thoughts here on dreams in the second category described above. And even so, I feel sure Haydn would not want any of his personal dreams or interpretations of those dreams to be given validity except as person-al views, conscious that these may be colored and influenced, to at least some degree, by the mind of the dreamer.

During his journey through cancer, Haydn had several dreams that were vivid and clearly symbolic. He shared these with me, I would write them down, and we would often discuss them to try to better understand their meaning and purpose. Neither of us have any skills in dream interpretation, any more than we had any prior skills or preparation for climbing the mountain we faced. In each case, our strategy was to take one step at a time and be open to the feedback guidance it gave us. I thought of this like sending a rocket to the moon. If we relied on perfect alignment at launch, no rocket would ever reach the moon. Yet the process of trajectory adjustment along the way, based on feedback guidance, makes the impossible possible, as rockets do indeed reach the moon. Feedback guidance is an essential tool for reaching our goals in life and for understand-ing the marvelous world of dreams.

—⁓—

At twenty-three years old, René Descartes, the French-born philoso-pher, mathematician, and scientist, had three dreams during the night of November 10, 1619. This was the culmination of preceding days and weeks of concern and anguish with the search for truth, and those dreams influenced Descartes' life's work in geometry, the mathematics of music, physics, metaphysics, and philosophy. He considered dreams as gifts from on high, and he took the time to write them down and interpret them in some detail. In his own in-terpretation of the three dreams, Descartes proposed that the whole of science, indeed the whole of knowledge, could be unified and illuminated by the method of *reason*. Indeed, Descartes is considered to have been a key instrument in heralding the Age of Reason.

Perhaps history's greatest and most prolific inventor—with an as-tounding 1,093 patents, including the electric lightbulb and the moving picture camera—Thomas Edison was well known to have a conflicted and contemptuous relationship with sleep and dreams. He was so driven by his work that he wrote in 1921 that he only slept "four or five hours a day." He relied on short but regular cat naps, and he had napping cots throughout his property, from labs to libraries. There are even several photographs of Edison napping outdoors. He napped to recharge. Although in his diary he denied having dreams, Edison experimented with dreamlike states experienced as a person falls asleep and as he awakens. How these "between states," respectively called hypnagogic and hypnopompic, can influence creativity is the subject of current research at the Uni-versity of Cambridge as well as other respected universities. Edison's experiment with hypnagogia didn't have the benefit of modern neu-roscience or equipment like functional MRIs, but it included the following four steps: first, relax and get quiet in a comfortable chair; second, hold a small steel ball in your hand; third, start sleeping, relax your grip, and drop the ball onto a steel surface or plate;

fourth, wake up and immediately record what you dreamed or experienced. Edison claimed that these experiments, sometimes assisted by his staff, helped him develop new ideas or work through existing problems.

Niels Bohr, the famous Danish atomic physicist, made some of the most innovative and groundbreaking contributions to understanding atomic structure and quantum mechanics. He accredited his discovery of the structure of the atom to an inspirational dream that led to this discovery. In his dream, he saw electrons spinning around the atom's nucleus like planets revolving around the sun. Bohr had previously struggled with various alternative frameworks for the configuration of the atom, but none would fit. When he awoke from his dream, Bohr felt that the vision in his dream was accurate and immediately began his search for the scientific evidence to support this new model of the atom. He won the Nobel Prize in Physics in 1922.

Albert Einstein was a contemporary of Niels Bohr. As an adolescent Einstein had a vivid dream about cows being electrocuted, which became the seed for his theory of relativity. Einstein took sleep and its benefits seriously, reportedly sleeping for ten hours per day—nearly one and a half times more than today's average American (6.8 hours). Like Edison, he also took regular but short naps.

There are numerous other great inventions and radical breakthroughs in the sciences and the arts that are attributed to dreams. Vincent Van Gogh famously said, "I dream my painting and I paint my dream." Even in politics, Mahatma Gandhi's idea of calling for a day of nonviolent protest and fasting—the famous "hartals," or mass strikes, of 1919 that were turning points during India's fight for self-determination—came to him in a dream.

There is a burgeoning increase in studies to test the theory that we can discover the realities of things and solve problems while sleeping, particularly during the REM phase associated with vivid dreaming. In 2004, a simple experiment conducted by scientists at the University of Lubeck, Germany, trained volunteers to play a number game. Most participants gradually improved with practice, but the fastest way to improve was to uncover a hidden rule. When the participants of the study were tested eight hours later, those who had been allowed to sleep were more than twice as likely to have insight into the hidden rules than those who had remained awake.

While Haydn's approach to dreams was not as rigorously analytical as Descartes', or as scientific as Edison's, Einstein's, or Bohr's, he enjoyed engaging with his dreams. He maintained an exploring and open mind in terms of what his dreams might mean, and he often found them to be a source of learning and laughter. As we climbed, our dreams became maps from the mountains, gifts to guide the way, if only we knew how to interpret them.

—⁜—

It is widely accepted that dreams are a manifestation of the unconscious mind. Some believe that the unconscious mind has a relationship with the spiritual soul or is an attribute of the soul. Because the language of the dream is that of the unconscious, its primary vocabulary and syntax is abstract or metaphoric, rather than the literal language of our material being. Just as we learn any language, we can also learn the language of dreams to understand and appreciate them. Dreams are a type of communication but are more than just communication; they are a process of bringing the contents of the subconscious into conscious awareness. In the words of Carl Jung, "Until you make the unconscious conscious, it will direct your life and you will call it fate."

Jung was the world's foremost authority on interpreting dreams by applying the method of science. When he was talking with a client, Jung started with the position that he didn't know anything more than the client. The dream is a mystery and should be approached with a degree of humility. The psychologist who thinks they understand the dream cannot understand the dream. The only way to understand it is to interact with it, to let it tell its own story. You must listen to the story and explore it together. With Jung's patients, after they went through the preliminary patient history, details, facts, and figures, they were ready to interact with and converse with the unconscious. The next week they would meet again; there would likely be a new dream, and the dialogue would continue. As the psychoanalyst in the room, Jung accompanied his patient's attempts to decode their dreams, letting themselves be guided by it while respecting dreams as being one step ahead, guiding the way. This attitude to interpreting dreams accepts that the unconscious is trying to help us understand something we don't understand—perhaps because of conscious prejudices or what society tells us we can or can't do or think or whatever set of limitations that the conscious is subject to. The dream tries to bypass the roadblocks that the conscious mind puts in our way.

Jung believed that it was possible to read a dream on the literal level and get one interpretation and read it on the symbolic level and get another. One can also read it on the individual level of the dreamer, on the level of the collective unconscious, or as a larger archetype of human existence. In other words, the dream is such a complex phenomenon that it can be valid and understood at all these different levels. The only way to understand the dream is therefore to interact with it. In a similar way, the story of the mountain unfolds only as one scales it. Just as the climb is an extraordinary conversation of the climber with the mountain, so, too, the learning we achieve through our dreams is made possible through the profound conversation between the dreamer and the dream.

Dreams remind us that the subject of the dream, the "me" who is experiencing the dream, is the spiritual me rather than the physical me. On waking from the dream, the two "me's" can have a conversation and become one. When this becomes a habit, we can live more coherent lives, informed by the richness and wonders of the dream world, while living purposefully in this world.

—∿—

On February 4, ten days after his first chemotherapy began in New York, and fifteen weeks before he left this world, Haydn had a particularly poignant dream. This is how he described it:

I was in a large boat that was sinking, standing in the hull of the ship, looking at two gaping holes in the sides of the ship where water gushed in.

We managed to get into a life raft, more like a long canoe, where I talked with someone about how my friend, Saeed, understood the physics of hull depth and other factors that might explain why the ship was sinking. The person I was with also wondered how we would fix the damaged canoe, as this also had a hole and was sinking. To properly guide the canoe to where we wanted, this began a pretty surreal scene, where our canoe dipped underwater, like it also had a hole in its hull and was going down. Suddenly, I had Aquaman-like powers and was underwater, pushing the canoe so it wouldn't crash into the ocean floor. I guided the canoe upwards and towards the shore. There, safely on the beach, we all thought we could camp out and use the canoe as a shelter.

Meanwhile I saw other groups of people, including Ashley, on a yacht enjoying themselves, and two or three of them rode a Jet Ski. When we arrived on the island, we realized we weren't the only ones there. It was a beautiful island, with white sands, clear water, and a breathtaking sense of calm and beauty. Ashley and her friends rode their Jet Ski onto the beach. There were many other groups of people along the beach, arriving in various ways. I am not entirely sure about this; it was just an impression I got that not everyone arrived by the same means.

In the final scene, my friend Luc arrived with a backpack and shades on. I got the impression that Luc arrived by helicopter; he was relaxed and at ease. He began to walk up this staircase, surrounded on both sides by beautiful greenery, like in Sanya. I hadn't previously noted the staircase, but it all seemed very beautiful and luxurious.

*The scene ends with Luc walking into the camera shot and me at the
base of the stairs ready to follow him up. I got the impression everyone
on the beach was ready to follow up the stairs after him and after me. I
never actually went up the stairs; he walked into the shot, filling the
frame, shot from the top of the staircase, and the dream ended.*

Haydn felt this was an important dream and was keen to find its
message. Although we talked a little, it was he who found his own
interpretation. These were his personal and unvarnished notes:

- Main hull of big boat had two massive holes with water
  pouring in . . . two failed treatments? Two areas of cancer
  not stemmed by the crazy rush of water? Etc.
- Little canoe is this lifeline we were given in NYC. . . . I
  relate Saeed to stem cells cuz his brother had this.
- It will seem like it's sinking as well but by some miraculous
  way will still lead us to the beautiful beach.
- Beach signifies enlightenment.
- Everyone on that beach has received their enlightenment
  and understanding in different forms of arrival (canoe, Jet
  Ski, helicopter, etc.).
- I was able to help everyone on our canoe to receive
  enlightenment and trust more in God through my story
  and the emails that we send out, etc.

At the time of this dream, things seemed to be looking up, and
we were hopeful, as were the doctors. When Haydn shared this
dream, I assumed that the canoe represented his body, as is often
the case with vehicles in dreams. I also thought that bringing the
canoe safely to shore was a hopeful sign that the treatments in New
York would be successful and would enable Haydn to return to a
beautiful life with his friends.

Following Haydn's passing, I reflected further on his notes of this
dream. It is conspicuous that there is no mention of dying or not

dying. It seems that Haydn was more concerned about helping others, especially to attain spiritual "enlightenment and understanding in different forms" than whether he was going to live or die. This dream was perhaps a sign that he would be given the strength to use his cancer (the sinking canoe) to help others find themselves and make it to the shores of true understanding.

At the time of this dream, I was not aware that in dream interpretation, at least in the category of interpretive dreams, it is commonly believed that the people in our dreams are all aspects of ourselves rather than separate individuals. If I had known this, I might have asked Haydn what associations came to his mind regarding Ashley or Luc, or any of us who might have featured in his dreams. Alas, I missed that moment.

—ɯ—

After Haydn passed away, I noticed that he appeared in several dreams to friends and family around the world. I hoped that Karyn and I would also see him in our dreams. Yet he didn't immediately appear in a dream to Karyn, the most obvious and closest person to him. After some months, I did have a particularly potent dream about Haydn. In my morning meditations following this dream, I felt clear that we receive dreams based on our needs, not our wants. If Jung was right, our dreams, or at least dreams that are not simply the chemical consequence of what we eat before going to bed, are a way of our unconscious balancing out all that is going on inside our lives. Dreams can serve as a corrective and balancing mechanism if we can only learn how to read and heed them. I suspect that in most cases, dreams that come from our unconscious are based upon our needs rather than on our wants, or our conscious and willful choices. They are gifts to guide our steps up the mountains before us, and we would do well to receive them as gifts and meditate on them. That would make sense to me then, that while Karyn would surely want to have a dream in which she could see her beloved Haydn, perhaps to be reassured of his happiness and peace, she may not actually need that because she is so clear in her very core that he is happy and at peace.

We might say that the purpose of our lives here is to become masters of our wants rather than to let our wants master us. If we don't master this, and surely it is a process without end, we might become slaves to our wants. I wonder whether dreams are a self-correction mechanism to assist us to be more aware of our wants, to better understand them, and to eventually get closer to mastering them. Thereby the me in my dreams is not my body, which of course is fast asleep in its bed, but the spiritual me who is having a human experience designed to help my progress and development. An important part of that development is to understand the difference between our needs and wants, to live ever mindful of the relationship between them, and to seek to master our wants so that they are not controlling us, especially if that is at the expense of other people's needs. This call for coherence, a profoundly private act of conscience, is beautifully expressed in the words of the international governing council of the Bahá'í community, in a letter dated March 1, 2017:

> *Every choice a Bahá'í makes—as employee or employer,*
> *producer or consumer, borrower or lender, benefactor or*
> *beneficiary—leaves a trace, and the moral duty to lead a*
> *coherent life demands that one's economic decisions be in*
> *accordance with lofty ideals, that the purity of one's aims be*
> *matched by the purity of one's actions to fulfill those aims.*
> —THE UNIVERSAL HOUSE OF JUSTICE

—m—

If Jung is correct, the world of dreams is the closest we may get to experiencing the wonder of the afterlife. As Jung wrote, "In dreams we put on the likeness of that more universal, truer, more eternal man dwelling in the darkness of primordial night. There he is still the whole, and the whole is in him, indistinguishable from nature and bare of all ego-hood." My personal understanding of the after-life is that there we are free of our ego and our free will—at least in the way we understand it here. If that is the case, the souls of those who have moved on are in a condition of progress that is akin to the rosebud flowering into the rose, or the almond tree in the famous haiku:

> I asked the almond tree,
> "O sister, tell me of God!"
> And the almond tree blossomed.

So when a loved one who has passed on appears in a dream, perhaps it is not because they are intentionally choosing to do so, in the same way we may make a conscious choice which of our family or friends we visit for a cup of tea, or just to "chill." That soul appears in our dream because it is what we need at that time. As we interact with our dreams, we may find it holds just that cup of tea we need to refresh and rebalance.

A man is not learned because he talks much; he who is patient, free from hatred and fear, he is called learned.

—THE DHAMMAPADA, 258

Be strong and of a good courage, fear not, nor be afraid of them: for the LORD thy God, he it is that doth go with thee; he will not fail thee, nor forsake thee.

—DEUTERONOMY 31:6 (KJV)

Armed with the power of Thy name nothing can ever hurt me, and with Thy love in my heart all the world's afflictions can in no wise alarm me.

—BAHÁ'U'LLÁH, *Prayers and Meditations*, 122.3

10.

FEAR

"Danger is real, but fear is a choice."

••••••••••••••••••••••••••••••••••

AWAITING AN URGENT BLOOD AND PLATELET TRANSFUSION IN THE busy ER of the Toronto General Hospital, Haydn turned to his mother and said, "Gosh, I could die in here." A stunned Karyn looked at him and exclaimed, "Haydn!" Calmly turning to Karyn, he replied, "Mom, this is a real possibility, so you shouldn't be afraid of it." Haydn's only real fear during his cancer journey was that the family who had so remarkably and generously agreed to sponsor his medical bills would feel their money had been wasted. He exemplified the idea that danger is real, but fear is a choice.

There is much fear in the world today, and apparently increasingly so. We are going through tempestuous times, engulfed by crises of every kind: environmental, social, political, economic, and spiritual. If the rising tide of hopelessness and despair, loneliness and depression, fear and anger, separation and disunity are signs of a spiritual crisis, then this may be the most underestimated of the current global crises in terms of severity and long-term prospects. In Chinese, the word for *crisis* (危機, or wēijī) is made by combining the Chinese characters for *danger* (危) and *opportunity* (機). I am hopeful that we can indeed find ways forward and opportunities to learn from the current crises to create a brilliant future. Alas, the fear that often paralyses us is very real.

Mountains are places of awesome majesty and beauty. They are also places of great danger, capable of provoking great fear. I remember a physics teacher from high school, an avid mountaineer, who came into class one day wearing a shoulder immobilizer sling. During school holidays, he had been climbing in the Alps and slipped, free falling down an ice chasm. Miraculously, he managed to hook his ice pick and stop his fall. In so doing, his right shoulder dislocated entirely. Dangling in midair, suspended by a rope, and in excruciating pain, Mr. Parker had the wherewithal and the strength to put his shoulder back into its socket before being pulled to safety by other members of the climb team. Standing in front of the class, he told this story and wisely commented something to the effect that echoes inspirational speaker Dan Meyer's TED Talk: "Danger is real, but fear is a choice."

On the heart-wrenchingly awful day of January 10, we sat with Haydn in a small consulting room at the hospital and were told that there was no hope of a cure. The doctors seemed stunned by this nineteen-year-old who thanked them, assured them that all would be okay, and didn't fear death. In these moments, I realized how intimate one's relationship is with fear. There I sat, hearing the same news, and I found myself stunned by fear's sudden punch—fear of what was to come and the levels of suffering, and fear of this physical world without Haydn. Karyn managed with grace to travel a profound journey from fear to strengthened faith. Her journey through fear offered a guiding beacon for me, as we navigated this storm. Her words:

> From the moment the call came, in that Singapore hotel room, I was ravaged by fear. So paralyzed, I don't remember how I packed my things, so stunned that I have no recollection now of even boarding the plane. For the next two weeks after our arrival in Canada, I feigned calm, for Haydn's sake. I maintained the outward appearance of control, while that fear raged within, ravaging my body, choking my breath. I eventually realized that it was depleting me completely, robbing me of

the very love and joy I so desperately wanted to give my son. That realization was a turning point for me, and I remember just when it took place.

I was in Toronto, in another hotel room, at the end of a very long day at the hospital. I found myself sitting on the edge of the bed at that moment, unable even to swallow a few leaves of salad. Fear was consuming me and I simply broke down. I wept uncontrollably, choked out prayers through my tears, and as I was literally gasping for air, I suddenly realized something very simple. If I claimed to have faith, then now must surely be the time to show it. If I believed in God, then now was the moment to accept His will, whatever it might be. I understood my fear was a test and I was being challenged by it to become detached. Haydn had been given to me not as a possession, not as a right, but as a trust from God. He belonged ultimately to God, and not to me.

At that moment I saw what "trust in God" actually looked like in my situation. It meant that whatever the outcome, Haydn would be fine. This realization opened a space for me and allowed me to be with him fully, to accompany him fearlessly and with faith from then on. In one of the Bahá'í prayers we ask God to protect us "from violent tests." To me, this doesn't mean we won't be tested; we need tests to grow. And I was surely tested as a mother through the awful ordeal of Haydn's illness. But during those two weeks when I lived in a state of fear rather than faith, I experienced the full impact of those violent tests. As long as I had not taken a conscious step into faith, I was not protected. All love and joy were depleted, and I could not truly be with Haydn.

I've come to understand that fear and faith cannot coexist in the same heart, or the same mind. Knowing that we are in God's hands and believing that He knows what is best for us enables us to accept the severe trials in life without fear, and helps us face the worst that might happen, confident that we will never be tested beyond our capacity. After that, my faith became my constant companion and solace. And Haydn became even more to me than he already was.

"Knowing that we are in God's hands," however, is not the same as knowing where the hand of destiny is leading us. That great unknown is beyond us and demands yet another leap of faith. When Haydn passed away, we were greatly comforted by a beautiful letter that was sent by 'Abdu'l-Bahá to a grieving mother who had lost her son in the prime of his youth. In this letter, 'Abdu'l-Bahá explains that:

> *It is as if a kind gardener transferreth a fresh and tender shrub from a confined place to a wide-open area. This transfer is not the cause of the withering, the lessening or the destruction of that shrub; nay, on the contrary, it maketh it to grow and thrive, acquire freshness and delicacy, become green and bear fruit. This hidden secret is well known to the gardener, but those souls who are unaware of this bounty suppose that the gardener, in his anger and wrath, hath uprooted the shrub. Yet to those who are aware, this concealed fact is manifest, and this predestined decree is considered a bounty. Do not feel grieved or disconsolate. . . .* [1]

I feel that faith in the afterlife is a remarkably powerful tool to conquer fear of death. When I was around nineteen, I read *Life After Life,* the bestselling book by Raymond A. Moody, documenting his extensive research into life after death through interviews with fifty survivors of near-death experiences (NDE). More recent books by well-respected medical doctors who have themselves had NDEs include *Proof of Heaven,* by Eben Alexander, and *To Heaven and Back,* by Mary C. Neal. But there remain materialists who are skeptical and question whether the afterlife is a serious field of scientific enquiry. Notwithstanding, even for those who posit that NDEs are hallucinations of the dying brain, it remains a mystery why so many of the stories contain similar features.

In his article "The Science of Near-Death Experiences" published in *The Atlantic,* Gideon Lichfield acknowledges, speaking of himself, "Even a hard-core materialist can learn a great deal from NDEs about how people make sense of the things that happen to them, and above all, about the central role that the stories we tell play in shaping our sense of who we are."[2]

More recently, Karyn and I met two separate friends who have both had NDEs, one of them twice. This is what that friend shared with us:

> *If we really knew what the afterlife was like, if we really believed in an afterlife, what life was for and what we are, and if we understood what the next world truly was, we would not have fear. Because we would feel we belong in our lives, and we would know that everyone else belongs in our life. . . . Regardless of who you are and what life you've lived, regardless of what you believe or do not believe, the Light (of the next world) is irresistible. Love is conveyed so instantly that it permeates every part of your awareness.*

In the scriptures of the world's religions, there is a consistent message: that the only healthy fear is the fear of God. This frees us from all other fears that may paralyze us and prevent us from living happy and healthy lives. To do so, the fear of God cannot also be paralyzing or incapacitating—for then it would have no use at all. From my own reading of scripture, the fear of God is the other side of the coin that is the love of God. Fear of God is not trepidation but the fear that His love might be withheld or that we may not be able to experience its life-giving power, which animates and sustains all of life.

It is no surprise that fear of God and love of God go hand in hand in the world's spiritual teachings. This fear is perhaps more akin to awe, respect, and reverence. For the skillful fisherman, fear of the ocean coexists with love of the ocean. For the skillful mountaineer, fear of the mountain coexists with love of the mountain. Fear shouldn't freeze us in our tracks or prevent our growth. Rather it can be cultivated into respect, to help us put our trust in those tracks, into courage to create new ones where needed, and into the knowledge that when we maintain the fixed ropes and their bolts, they will hold us, without fail, if we fall.

—ᵐ—

A tool that both Karyn and I found very helpful in dealing with fear was to continually remind ourselves that things could have been far worse. This simple tool helped immensely. We had the bounty of spending 24/7 with Haydn. He was within sight and within reach. How much worse it would have been for us if he had been kidnapped or estranged? Not knowing and not being able to connect to our child would have been far worse for us. At least we had the good fortune of loving him and of receiving his love and wisdom, witnessing his courage, accompanying him to the veil, being grateful for the most wonderful nineteen years we had together, and rejoicing in his many beautiful qualities and abundant life.

Hilary Hinton "Zig" Ziglar was an American author and motivational speaker who experienced several tragedies in his life but had a special ability to see these in a positive light. He is accredited with the saying: "F-E-A-R has two meanings: 'Forget Everything and Run' or 'Face Everything and Rise.' The choice is yours."

Fear is natural. There is nothing to be ashamed of or to deny if our first reaction is fear, for our loved ones or people who are vulnerable or isolated. What I am suggesting is that we can meet fear and subdue it, just as we can stand tall and meet any of our mountains. As with our lesson regarding faith, the process is first "to know"—to authentically accept the emotion, maybe to even begin to understand its origins or trigger points—and then "to do," or to work with it. In climbing the mountain, we must move one step at a time. Two steps forward, three steps back, is still to move. Movement, taking informed action and/or intentional choices, quells feelings of fear.

Part of the context of fear is that it is often a reaction. I have come to realize, from my own experiences of fear, that it is possible to consciously shift gears from being *reactive*—whether to people, situations, or our own anxieties—to being simply *active*. One can make that shift through meditation, prayer, or free will that is then applied and tested in baby steps—consciously choosing to step out of fear and to stand instead in one's authority, in a place where we can observe the fear, without feeling crushed or terrified because of it.

According to Eckhart Tolle, fear in this world can be overcome by "turning up the Presence." Fear is only a fear-filled thought. You are not the thought. In Tolle's terminology, "You are the Presence that witnesses the fearful thought. So, you don't have to believe what the thought is telling you. Just let it be there. When you stand in your Presence, you don't feed the thought, and it loses its power over you."[3]

Some observers note that when one has lost everything—whether by war, famine, disaster, or losing a loved one—at that moment any fear one may have previously held gives way to a feeling of deep peace, serenity, and complete freedom from fear. I experienced this at the very instant Haydn took his last breath. If an army of ten thousand men had entered our home in that moment, I was detached. There was not an ounce of fear or trepidation, not a dot of anxiety nor worry. I felt empty of everything except the most potent and serene love, for Haydn, for family, for God. In that moment I may have tasted what St. Paul referred to in the Bible's book of Philippians when he described, "the peace of God which passeth all understanding."

—⁂—

Fear is usually associated with danger or imminent loss and generally with the unknown outcomes of either. Conscious knowledge of what is happening or going to happen may be sufficient to assuage the fear. Whether danger or loss, or both, the concern is usually material—that something terrible will happen to us or our loved ones—that we may be hurt, killed, or endangered.

If the fear associated with material danger or loss can be overcome by standing strong in the awareness of our spiritual core, then what about fear that is associated with spiritual danger or loss? One might say that this is the only valid fear because it has much more serious consequences. If we lose our spiritual awareness, we lose the anchor that protects us in times of material danger or loss. So, fear of God or fear of displeasing God, which is advocated in all the major faith traditions, is healthy and keeps us alive to who we really are, our essential or spiritual reality. Metaphorically, it also keeps us on our toes and protects the egoistic self from puffing up and getting out of control. One can't have a raging ego and a genuine fear of God at the same time. Fear of God is an essential quality of the nurtured human soul. It protects us from our self, or at least our insistent self.

So what happens when we see ourselves first and foremost as spiritual beings that are having a material experience rather than as material beings having a spiritual experience? First, we have a powerful vantage point from which to observe and handle the fear of losing a material possession, even it is our favorite thing—whether that be a book, a treasure, even a limb, or our body itself. Such a material loss is no longer so terrible if we are spiritual beings that continue to exist independently of the material world we are presently passing through. Even losing our physical life is not the end of our reality, identity, or true life as a spiritual being. When we continually anchor ourselves in this spiritual truth of who we really are, whether one calls this the "soul" or our "presence," we notice those moments of fearfulness. For example, with a burglar in the house, or a snake in the car, or a cancer in one's head, we stand firm and calm in the assurance that the house, car, or even our own body, is not "me." The real "me," the soul, is a noble and eternal reality that cannot be hurt by any burglar, snake, or cancer. Let the real "me" be the reality that observes the burglar, snake, or cancer and know that however fierce the attack—whether imaginary or real—the soul is above and beyond this material world and is unassailable, sacrosanct, and safe.

The only condition for such assured protection is that we nurture this soul so that we can actually take refuge there, knowing we are safe and strong in who we really are. The writings of the holy books describe the soul as a reflection of God, a mirror of His attributes, a sign of His knowledge, and that the human soul—each one of us unique and indescribably beautiful—is held in the hand of God. From such a vantage point, what is there to fear? The most violent burglar, the most poisonous snake, or the most incurable disease are all material tests. They are all temporary and temporal. They will all pass. The soul goes on, irresistibly and forever moving toward its Beloved.

approaching
the summit

What four things lead to distinction? Four kinds of detachment:
detachment from the bonds of sensuality, desire for rebirth, views, and
ignorance.

—Dīghanikāya: Long Discourses 1, XXXIV:4.7

You came here empty-handed, and you will leave empty-handed.

—Sri Krishna, The Bhagavad Gita

As for goods and possession, the great man does not compete for them.

—Zhuangzi, chapter 17

11.

DETACHMENT

"You are not your body!"

IN LATE FEBRUARY, WHILE HE WAS STILL QUITE MOBILE, HAYDN played the board game Settlers of Catan with his siblings and a friend. At some point, the group took a short break, during which I found myself shoulder to shoulder with Haydn as we stood together in the kitchen. Haydn seemed excited as he shared that, during the game, he made a discovery. He realized that happiness is so often associated with getting what we want. And in a board game, when not everyone can win, or when a sibling has just stolen a knight or spoiled a plan, it's easy to become unhappy or at least a little disappointed. So he started playing with no expectations. From this simple experiment that he was conducting, he realized that detachment from results is a wonderful way to assure happiness, whatever the outcome.

This seemingly obvious lesson is a vital nugget among many that this journey has taught us. It was a delight to hear Haydn share this moment of realization. One might have thought from his excitement that he had discovered gravity or that the proverbial apple had fallen on his head. In hindsight, it had, for this was no less valuable a discovery.

Haydn and his siblings were all born and raised in China. Although they were raised in a Bahá'í family, they had friends and classmates from diverse backgrounds and beliefs. In their class-rooms and in the neighborhood, people came from a range of faith backgrounds—Hindu, Buddhist, Jewish, Christian, Muslim, Mormon, and Bahá'í—as well as from families that were atheist or agnostic.

The majority of our friends were mainland Chinese, whose parents were raised in Communist China without religious education or affiliation. That is not to say that they were not spiritual. In many cases they were profoundly spiritual, only without the labels and the trappings of religious traditions. Chinese culture is infused with a unique blend of spiritual teachings from Buddhism, Taoism, and Confucianism. Although Chinese socialism derived from nine-teenth-century Marxism and twentieth-century communism, and was most poignantly expanded through the teachings and rule of Chairman Mao, it did not destroy the deep spiritual roots of Chinese culture—although it certainly tried during the Cultural Revolution (1964–74), which was not the first cultural revolution in Chinese history. Chinese culture is remarkably deep rooted and resilient, and we were grateful that our children grew up in China and learned from its wisdom. One of the core concepts in Chinese culture is detachment, as we may recall from the "Maybe yes, maybe no" story in chapter 2.

Taught by the Buddha more than twenty-five hundred years ago, the Four Noble Truths of Buddhism were his first teachings after receiving enlightenment. They form the basis of Buddhist philoso-phy. The second Noble Truth states that the cause of suffering is attachment. In other words, we suffer because we cannot bear to let go of things, ideas, and expectations. The third Noble Truth is that it is possible to end suffering. To do that we have to accept reality for what it is. Knowing that everything in life comes and goes, we must, as far as possible, relinquish our attachments to relieve our individ-ual suffering. Buddhists use attachment as another word for expec-tations. Attachment is the trap we fall into time and time again. For example, we get attached to feelings, such as euphoria and excitement; we get attached to experiences, especially as a substitute for relationships; we get attached to stories, some of which are unfounded mind talk, which we retell over and over again in our minds; and instead of living in the present, we overly attach to the past or the future.

In 2008, Beijing hosted one of the most memorable and impressive Olympics. One day, we took the children to watch one of the Paralympic events at the Bird's Nest stadium. When we alighted from the train at the subway station, we were excited and eager to get to the event. Halfway up one of the crowded escalators, Karyn turned back to me and asked, "Where's Haydn?" In that moment, moving in a human sea, both in front and behind us, our hearts sank. How could we possibly have lost one of the children? Haydn was eight-years-old at the time and nowhere to be seen. I instinctively turned and ran down the upward moving escalator, against the tide of people, which somehow managed to part sufficiently to let me through. I called Haydn's name at the top of my voice as I retraced our steps to find him. My heart pounded so strongly I could hear it, although I can't rationalize how that could be possible in such a noisy place as a Beijing subway station during the Olympics.

While I haven't read this anywhere in Chinese wisdom, there are times when it helps to stand out—in this case being a tall white guy, with a loud voice, in a crowd in China. Perhaps a minute or so later, a group of Chinese in the crowd moving toward me started pointing toward the top of the escalator. I will never forget the sheer relief as I saw Haydn standing there, even though he was crying and quite shaken. Twelve years later, preparing to say farewell to our beloved Haydn, I recalled this traumatic incident. Perhaps, in a small way, it helped prepare me for the eventual detachment I would need in order to accept life as a family without his physical presence.

—m—

In many places, the scriptures of the past teach us to practice detachment in order to live happily. In my opinion, detachment is especially valuable to deal with the tests and trials of life, including illness, whether physical, mental, or emotional.

One day, Haydn received a very touching note and video message from a young man who had been struggling with MS for several years. He was living in Wales and had never met Haydn, but his wife had dinner with us in Beijing several years earlier and had heard that Haydn was unwell. Haydn shared the video with me and then repeated a phrase that he heard from this young man, who had looked straight into the video camera and shared the wise and timely insight, "You are not your body!"

This phrase became a real comfort for Haydn. It was also a reminder that acts of kindness and compassion to the sick and suffering, especially messages or visits from friends, can be a gift that keeps on giving. In dealing with illness, it is essential to be detached from the disease, or one can lose faith and hope quickly. That advice applies especially to the patient but also to caregivers. For family members, when we saw Haydn's hands shaking, or his legs giving way, or moments of confusion at the very end of his life, we reminded ourselves that this was the disease, not Haydn. We detached and separated the two. This simple but important realization removes the desire or inclination to correct. By separating the person from the disease, we are likely to be more understanding, more forgiving, and more supportive.

In illness, the body is stricken by a disease that prevents or interferes with its healthy functioning. We do well to remind ourselves, especially if we see that weakened, damaged, or frail body, that it is just a body that is afflicted. The reality of the person who inhabits that body, or, more precisely, the soul that is associating with that body, is quite separate and far greater. The illness of the body doesn't imply the illness of the soul. The relationship of the body to the soul is a mystery. I have found some of the most powerful insights into this relationship through considering the metaphor of the earth's relationship to the sun. The earth would cease to exist without the life-giving power of the sun. However, the sun would be entirely unaffected if earth ceased to exist. So too, the body cannot exist without the life-giving power of the human soul; however, the soul is independent of all conditions of the body and is therefore unaffected by the illness or death of the body. If one were to address the wholeness of the universe, earth and sun included, and say, "You are not the earth!" this would be correct.

One of the most valuable benefits of mindfulness training, particularly from meditation, is not only the awareness that you are not your body but that you are also not your thoughts, or even your emotions. Imagine yourself sitting on the sofa watching television. Now imagine yourself being the one who is watching the person sitting on the sofa watching television. This is the shift that takes place in mindfulness, usually through the practice of meditation. Making this shift, away from the most obvious and the neediest "me" is a practice of detachment. It usually enables one to see the me on the sofa with greater clarity, by stepping back and changing one's vantage point. With such clarity one is better able to achieve radical and honest acceptance of the thoughts, struggles, and emotions associated with that me. Even more valuable is that such detachment enables one to see the untapped potential and the brilliance of that unique and noble human being sitting on the sofa, and to assist that being to get up and change the world for the better. Detachment is not a passive condition for monks in far-off monasteries; it is for soldiers, activists, athletes, mountaineers. It is for each and every one of us in the collective human family.

—⁂—

In chapter 3, we noted research showing that the radical acceptance of all our emotions is the cornerstone to thriving and authentic happiness. Detached acceptance applies the tools of science to accurately label our emotions rather than casually jumping to quick and easy tags. In doing so, we clarify our emotions by naming them. We are then ready to master our emotions rather than be enslaved by them. We move from the thought "I am sad," to "I notice my sadness." Along with "You are not your body!" is "You are not your sadness!" With this realization, combining the method of science with the spiritual practice of detachment, we are ready to address questions that will likely yield rich learning, such as, "What is my emotion telling me?" This is the *emotional agility* we encountered in chapter 2, now purified from any motives when we are *detached from the outcome*. We are now able to scale almost anything. That, for me, was one of Haydn's key messages.

Be fearless, joyful, and not attached to the outcome.

—ɯ—

Haydn had no appetite for conflict or contention. Rather he avoided these and was clear about doing so. If the need to be right against others who are wrong is an expression of the ego, then it would seem Haydn was a young man who was to an unusual degree in control of his ego, rather than vice versa. In reflecting on why he was able to light up a room, even when sick and having very little energy, I think it may have been his relative detachment from ego, from the insistent self that we all have to deal with. In observing Haydn with others, including us as his family, I noticed his sincere desire to see others succeed and rejoice in their successes. He took a genuine interest in people, seeing the good in them. He was able to light up a room, but not because it crossed his mind that he wanted to do so. He just did so naturally because he was easy to be with, a man who was comfortable in his own skin, with no need to prove himself and definitely no need to take from others or put anyone down.

However beautiful it may be, a lamp can light up a room only if it is plugged into an electricity source. And when it is, even a rather humble lamp may shine far more brightly than a larger more impressive lamp that is not actually plugged in but relying on itself to be noticed. The key point here is to be a conduit of the light rather than to focus on the lamp. Light is good in whatever lamp it shines.

—⁓—

As we further undertook what felt like a herculean effort of detachment—needing to let go of the life we dreamed for Haydn—meditation proved yet again a powerful tool. A dear family friend, known to Haydn as Uncle Roy, had always inspired us with his love for meditation as a daily spiritual practice. As early as the second week into Haydn's nine-and-a-half-month journey through cancer, Haydn asked Roy to help him meditate. Over the months, Roy made a series of recorded meditations that Haydn played regularly. These were calming and soothing, and they helped when he struggled to sleep. The meditations also guided Haydn through visualizing his healthy white cells bathed in light, slowly dissolving the tumor with each breath, or his bone marrow making new white blood cells and sending those into his body as soldier cells to protect him.

One of the most powerful of the visualizations Roy sent us involved seeing one's own body as an observer. In this guided meditation, one visualizes floating slowly to the top of the room, looking down on one's body, then floating further upward, so one can observe one's body from above the top of the building. As one continues to float upward, one sees not only the building but the street, then the neighborhood, eventually the entire city, then the province or state, the country and continent, and eventually the beautiful blue planet that is our earth home. From out in space, the journey then returns, step by step, slowly descending until one is back in the building and then in the room and finally in one's body again. The visualization concludes with feeling one's arms, one's torso, one's legs, feeling gratitude for everything that is given to us, for our connection to this beautiful planet, for our oneness with all humanity, for the gift of spirit, for the incredible infinite reality of God. In that space of wonder and gratitude, one rests a while, completely detached.

This "planet meditation," as we referred to it, reinforces the idea that "You are not your body!" and unleashes a sense of liberation and acceptance.

> *It is truly a great cosmic paradox that one of the best teachers in all of life turns out to be death. . . . While someone could tell you that you are not your body, death shows you.*
> —MICHAEL A. SINGER, *The Untethered Soul*

There is value in contemplating the afterlife, especially as a tool to practicing detachment in this life. Death is not some morbid subject to be avoided, nor is it healthy to sit around fixated by thoughts of an inevitable end, paralyzed by feelings of hopelessness. In *The Promulgation of Universal Peace*, 'Abdu'l-Bahá warns against the futile preoccupation with death that leaves us despondent and weakened:

> *The conception of annihilation is a factor in human degradation, a cause of human debasement and lowliness, a source of human fear and abjection. It has been conducive to the dispersion and weakening of human thought, whereas the realization of existence and continuity has upraised man to sublimity of ideals, established the foundations of human progress and stimulated the development of heavenly virtues; therefore, it behooves man to abandon thoughts of nonexistence and death, which are absolutely imaginary, and see himself ever-living, everlasting in the divine purposes of his creation.*

Fear of death is detrimental to our spiritual health and comes from an understanding of death simply as the body's physical demise. To overcome such fear, we need to reconceptualize death such that its ultimate insignificance in our spiritual journey becomes more and more apparent to us. Death is a great teacher, a great leveler, and provides an almost instant perspective that often eludes us in the ebb and flow of life. In *The Untethered Soul*, bestselling author Michael A. Singer writes:

It is death that makes life precious. Look how precious life becomes when you imagine you only have a week left to live. How precious would life be if there was no such thing as death? You'd waste every second of it because you'd figure you'd always have it. It is scarcity that makes things precious. It is scarcity that makes a simple rock become a rare gem. . . .

Don't be afraid of death. Let it free you. Let it encourage you to experience life fully. But remember, it's not your life. You should be experiencing the life that's happening to you, not the one you wish was happening. Don't waste a moment of life trying to make other things happen; appreciate the moments you are given. Don't you understand that every moment you are a step closer to death? This is how to live your life. You live it as though you were on the verge of death, because you are.

Like the planet meditation, contemplating the afterlife gives us a vantage point to see the forest rather than just the trees, or the mountain range rather than just the next mountain top. Contemplating the afterlife also expands our sense of time horizons and allows us to imagine our place in the greater scheme of things, in the ebb and flow of history, rather than just attending to our immediate needs and concerns. With such a perspective we are able to think longer, bigger, and wider. We are able to see ourselves in the grand context of humanity, rather than just of oneself, and of the whole world rather than just one's own world.

On one occasion the Buddha asked several of the monks, "How often do you contemplate death?" One of them replied, "Lord, I contemplate death every day." "Not good enough," the Buddha said and asked another monk, who replied, "Lord, I contemplate death with each mouthful that I eat during the meal." "Better, but not good enough," said the Buddha, "What about you?" The third monk said, "Lord, I contemplate death with each inhalation and each exhalation."

—Mahaparinibbana Sutta

It's a simple yet profound truth that without understanding death, we can't truly understand life. Death realigns our lives, nudges us to question our choices and evaluate how and where we choose to spend our time and energies. It also highlights the importance of our spiritual lives.

We tend to see life and death as opposites: one as the beginning, the other as the end. In reality, however, birth and death are both the beginnings of new chapters of life. They are also each the endings of the previous chapter. When a loved one passes away, we tend to offer our condolences to those they have left behind, trying to solace their grief by talking of the wonder and beauty of salvation, of heaven or paradise, or of being reunited with their God. Unfortunately, these well-intentioned vagaries are less consoling than we might imagine, as they speak of the afterlife as being something wholly unconnected to life and focus our attention on the fact that the deceased, as we knew them, is no more. Talking about life and the afterlife as two distinct and unrelated realms of existence does little to make death seem less tragic and final.

All world religions, in some form, describe death not as the end of life but as the beginning of a new stage in the infinite spiritual journey. Their scriptures, echoed by great thinkers such as the Jesuit priest Pierre Teilhard de Chardin, teach us, "We are not human beings having a spiritual experience. We are spiritual beings having a human experience." Human beings have both a material reality that is temporal and a spiritual reality that is eternal. Human life is not a finite period during which we walk this earth but rather one part of a spiritual journey that continues for all eternity. Death is merely the point along the path when the soul is released to take its flight and continue its eternal journey.

> *To consider that after the death of the body the spirit perishes is like imagining that a bird in a cage will be destroyed if the cage is broken, though the bird has nothing to fear from the destruction of the cage. Our body is like the cage, and the spirit*

is like the bird. We see that without the cage the bird flies in the world of sleep; therefore, if the cage becomes broken, the bird will continue and exist. Its feelings will be even more powerful, its perceptions greater, and its happiness increased.

—'Abdu'l-Bahá, *Some Answered Questions*

Surrender the grasping disposition of selfishness, and you will attain to that calm state of mind, which conveys perfect peace, goodness, and wisdom.

—SUTRA COLLECTION (RS), 57.18

Calm your anger and abandon wrath. Don't be angry—it only leads to evil.

—THE BOOK OF PSALMS, TEHILIM, 37:8

The best of wisdom, being calm and kind.

—IMAM ALI, *2500 Adages of Imam Ali*, 1.577

12.

CALM

"Be courageous. And don't do normous!"

IN LATE MARCH, AFTER HAYDN LEARNED THAT HIS CANCER HAD spread from his brain to his spine and was resistant to treatments, I sent the following update email:

> *On Monday evening, we went around the table and each shared what we thought were the gifts we had received during our two months in New York. Haydn shared that he felt grateful that he had "become stronger." Given his current prognosis, I took a double take before realizing that he was of course showing gratitude for the spiritual growth that is so tangible in this extraordinary young man. In the greater scheme of life in this world and "more abundant life" in the worlds to come, what else matters more?*

Haydn read widely and felt a connection to the Stoics, particularly Marcus Aurelius, Stoic philosopher and Roman emperor from 161 CE until his death in 180 CE. Aurelius was the last emperor of the Pax Romana, an age of relative peace and stability for the Roman Empire, although not without its crises—including the Antonine Plague of 165–180 CE. The famous historian Edward Gibbon wrote that under Marcus Aurelius, the last of the "Five Good Emperors," "the Roman Empire was governed by absolute power, under the guidance of wisdom and virtue." Today, we are left with *The Meditations*, Aurelius' personal journal most probably written while he was on campaign in central Europe c. 171–75 CE. It is organized into twelve books, providing a guideline on how to use reason and logic, how to control one's emotions, and how to achieve calm through self-mastery. Over and over, Aurelius reminds himself to detach his emotions from the difficulties of the world, to maintain his composure during tough times, and to treat all fates as equal—success and failure, prosperity and poverty, life and death. In his own words:

> *Objective judgment, now at this very moment. Unselfish action, now at this very moment. Willing acceptance—now at this very moment—of all external events. That's all you need.*

The Stoics used memento mori, an artistic or symbolic reminder of death, to invigorate life and create priority and meaning. They treated each day as a gift and reminded themselves constantly not to waste time on the trivial and vain. Aurelius famously wrote to himself: "You could leave life right now. Let that determine what you do and say and think." The emperor considered it imperative to keep death at the forefront of his thoughts, not to create panic but to inspire priority, humility, urgency, and appreciation. In doing so, the world's most powerful man of the time piloted the obligations of his position by living virtuously in the moment as it presented itself.

The Stoic philosophers of Greece and Rome—including Zeno, Seneca, Epictetus, and Marcus Aurelius—believed in the soul, in a divine cause to our existence, and in a life after death. In line with Stoic principles for living, they advocated cultivating virtue, detaching from the world's happenings, and promoting good citizenship. Stoics also valued maintaining a "Stoic calm," or a calm indifference to external events. No wonder Haydn felt a connection to the Stoics.

—〰—

On January 23, 2020, I sat in an Uber driving to the hospital in New York. The driver was a Nepalese Sherpa who had twice summited Everest. I asked him what he considered the most important quality of a great mountain climber. He replied, "Be courageous. And don't do normous!" After quizzing him a little further, I realized he was saying, "And don't be nervous!" Where there are steep precipices, hidden crevasses, and shifting glaciers, there is no room for fear, anxiety, or nervousness. Easier said than done. Thankfully, Haydn was a great climbing companion, who inspired us all through his gentle calm, kindness, and resilience.

As I reflect on our journey with Haydn, this particular lesson is one of the most poignant for me. At the time I heard this Nepalese wisdom, I was quick to pass it on to Haydn. In retrospect, I wish I had taken in more of the message myself. If I could wind back the clock and climb this mountain again, I would likely have served the family better had I been more calm and less nervous. Whenever we left the house for Haydn's appointments, I felt a need to get every single possible thing prepped and ready. Every detail seemed massively important—it must have appeared like I was heading off on a NASA mission! Yes, it may have seemed excessive, and I admit I had little patience if questioned, but these were the things I could control when immersed in such powerlessness. My anxiety caused unease among mature people who frankly didn't enjoy feeling micromanaged. Thankfully, Haydn and Karyn were able to exchange looks, smile, and keep calm. Things came to a head one day when Karyn insisted we go for a walk. We got to the end of the Brooklyn pier when she just wept in my arms, letting go of months of pent-up feelings of inadequacy due to my endless micromanagement. She questioned whether she was even useful. How awful that must have been for my partner in life and for a mother already going through this heart-shattering ordeal.

In writing this book, the subjects of these nineteen lessons were selected based on interviews with Haydn's family and friends. Ironically, they feel like exactly the medicine I also needed for our climb. In terms of remaining calmer, especially in times of duress, I would like to have worried less and trusted more. Several of this book's lessons—acceptance, positivity, faith, mindfulness, detachment—would have helped create more calm, whether in my body or in our home, through practice.

—✺—

Haydn's friend Chris wrote to us after Haydn's passing to share how much impact Haydn's calm and considerate manner had on his life. He wrote, "I never once heard Haydn raise his voice. He was always calm and composed even in the chaos that surrounded him. He thought about what he said, he thought of its impact. Even when he disagreed, he said so in a way that did not cause confrontation but reflection."

Late one night at the lake house, while Haydn was in bed eating spaghetti, Keyan turned to him and said, "Haydn, I've learned calm and courage from you. You have shown me what it means to be courageous, so if I ever have to go through this, I have your example. And I'm not afraid of dying anymore because you aren't."

The list goes on.

—✺—

One night, a few months after Haydn's passing, I had two dreams about him. In the first, which was in black and white, we played golf. Haydn appeared to be about fourteen or fifteen years old, and he hit a shot that went straight to the green, smoothly rolled toward the hole, and gently dropped into the cup. Until that moment, neither of us had seen an actual hole in one. I turned to Haydn, who smiled with a warm, easy, and joyous smile. There was no jumping up and down, no whooping and shouting—which is typical among even the most underrated of golfers. This was his first hole in one, even if in a dream! Haydn remained the essence of calmness. It was a beautiful moment.

Not long after, during the same night, I had a second dream, this time in color. In the second dream, we were again playing golf. Haydn hit a tee shot toward the green, and his ball looked like it was heading left of the hole. When it started to roll across the sloping green, it moved from left to right and stopped, perched on the lip of the hole. I held my breath, wondering if it would drop into the cup. I looked at Haydn. He stood totally still and completely calm. Stoic. I looked back at the green and saw that his ball had somehow climbed a little, so it was now sitting atop a tiny mound maybe an inch or so high, almost like a small ant hill, right on the edge of the hole. As I watched the mound, it softly crumbled and dropped the ball into the hole. Haydn looked up and, again, smiled. Two holes in one, in the same night!

As I lay in bed and wondered what this meant, I felt that the first dream was about Haydn's life before cancer. It was pretty "textbook," at least from the perspective of a proud parent. Haydn was the first to admit that he had a relatively privileged and happy life, blessed with good health, academic success, artistic and musical talents, and ample opportunities for international travel and exposure to diversity. He also had a loving family, supportive friends, and he found meaningful opportunities to be of service to society. Perhaps there was a reason why the first dream was in black and white and why the hole in one was the symbol of the dream. Lest anyone mistake this for boasting, God forbid, a hole in one is not achieved purely by merit. There is always more than a reasonable amount of luck or good fortune involved.

Maybe the second dream was about Haydn's journey through cancer. It was in color—life jolted into a new, less predictable world with all operating systems at high levels. The second dream reminded me of something I noticed a few days earlier. I spotted a black ant moving across a stone slab beside the pool. The ant seemed longer than normal, until I realized it was *two* ants. One ant was walking with its antennae outstretched, carrying the other ant in front of it. I didn't realize the ant being carried was dead until I saw the carrying ant go right to the edge of the pool, lean over, and gently drop its dead companion into the water. It was a sublime sight and not something I expected from one of the smallest and humblest of nature's creatures. This unassuming spectacle of nature evoked a similar sense of warmth and awe that I felt in the second dream. Perhaps it was a reminder of the gentle ease of Haydn's reaction to his cancer? Or that Haydn's calm demeanor was constant, regardless of which challenge he faced—whether the soccer team tryouts or his cancer journey? Did his characteristic calm strengthen over time, preparing him for this climb? Or did the climb itself strengthen the depth and inner resources of his calm? Was his calm due to nature or nurture? How much of this exquisite and inspiring quality was a gift or talent, and how much was it the result of his inner resolve and personal effort? Perhaps all of the above?

Haydn's last view over the ocean, Hamptons, New York; March 2020. *Photo courtesy of Pan Shiyi.*

The wise person, a giver of happiness—attains happiness himself.

—SUTRA COLLECTION (B), 16.2

Material progress insures the happiness of the human world. Spiritual progress insures the happiness and eternal continuance of the soul.

—'ABDU'L-BAHÁ, *Bahá'í World Faith*, 4.6

Happiness again results from the disease of desire being cured. From joy also springs sorrow, and hence sorrow arises repeatedly. Sorrow comes after joy, and joy after sorrow. The joys and sorrows of human beings are revolving on a wheel. After happiness sorrow has come to thee. Thou shalt again have happiness. No one suffers sorrow forever, and no one enjoys happiness forever. The body is the refuge of both sorrow and happiness.

—VYĀSA, THE MAHABHARATA 12, 175.6

13.

HAPPINESS

"Don't cry because it's over, smile because it happened." —Dr. Seuss

SINCE HE WAS A TODDLER, HAYDN WAS KNOWN FOR HIS CONTAGIOUS laugh, which echoed through his kindergarten in Beijing. Whether he was at the unity rug or running up the stairs between the toddler and primary classes, the laugh was there, even if he was just laughing on his own. It is now a treasure beyond treasures to have a recording of Haydn's early laugh on his kindergarten CD of songs.

At this kindergarten, the entrance wall was carved with the words "You live to do good and to bring happiness to others."[1] Those were also the lyrics for the school's graduation song for its five- and six-year-old graduates, including Haydn. Simple lessons with a significant impact, especially when taught at this age.

Haydn took this to heart in many ways throughout his years. He exhibited a profound delight in delivering happiness to others—truly, the more he gave the happier he became, at times even giddy with anticipation. When he became ill, this quality magnified. While lying sick and exhausted in hospital beds, he still made other people's wishes come true. Keyan was quite a fan of the TV show *The Office* and in particular of the actor Rainn Wilson, who played the role of Dwight Schrute. So Haydn discreetly arranged for Keyan to meet Rainn by phone. I remember the day that Haydn called him over to his bed and casually said, "This is a call for you." He handed Keyan the phone with Rainn Wilson at the other end.

Although best known as a comedic actor, Rainn regularly speaks out on social and spiritual issues. In his 2014 keynote speech for the USC baccalaureate ceremony, he shared, "Self-esteem, well-being, spiritual connectedness, life satisfaction, meaning, a sense of community—all these tangible things are experienced and brought to light by service to others. Volunteering, helping, showing kindness, sacrificing your time and energy, giving selflessly—these are the things that will give you the greatest human flourishing."[2]

"In this me-me-me culture," Rainn continued, "focus on yourself and you will find only misery, depression, emptiness. Focus on helping others and you will find joy, contentment, gratitude, happiness. . . . Ultimately, it is in giving to others that we will realize our greatest joy." As Rainn has often expressed, these are the same themes he, too, has found in the teachings of the world's religions.

> *The more we search for ourselves, the less likely we are to find ourselves. The more we search for God and try and serve our fellow men, the more profoundly we become acquainted with ourselves and the more inwardly assured. This is one of the great spiritual laws of life.*
> —SHOGHI EFFENDI, LIGHTS OF GUIDANCE, 391

—m—

Science has shown that one of the most effective causes of joy and happiness, or subjective well-being, is gratitude. Especially during the past twenty years of positive psychology research, numerous published studies have demonstrated that increased happiness is consistently associated with an attitude of gratitude. In one study, psychologists Robert A. Emmons of the University of California, Davis, and Michael E. McCullough of the University of Miami asked all participants to write a few sentences each week on defined topics. One group wrote about things they felt grateful for that had occurred during the week. The second group wrote about daily irritations or things that had displeased them. A third group wrote about events that had affected them but with no emphasis on whether these were positive or negative. After ten weeks, those who wrote about gratitude were more optimistic and felt better about their lives. Surprisingly, those in the "gratitude" group also exercised more and had fewer visits to physicians than those who focused on sources of aggravation.

Brother David Steindl-Rast, a Benedictine monk and interfaith scholar, echoed this message during his popular 2013 TED talk:

> *If you think it's happiness that makes you grateful, think again. It's gratefulness that makes you happy.*

Steindl-Rast writes and speaks about the "gentle power" of gratefulness:

> *Look closely and you will find that people are happy because they are grateful. The opposite of gratefulness is just taking everything for granted.*[3]

Gratitude is something that is taught and learned, rather than being innate. In kindergarten, we learn to say thank you to show our gratitude for a delicious snack, extra playtime, or for help completing small tasks such as tying a shoe. As we grow older, our sources of happiness, gratitude, and well-being may change, and we may be grateful for gifts of time, respect, lifelong friendships, or opportunities to serve others. While the major world religions have called us to gratefulness for centuries, the science of gratitude and the science of happiness are in their infancies. Happiness and gratitude may operate in a "cycle of virtue," whereby gratitude enhances happiness and happiness enhances gratitude.

In contemporary Western society, we are at risk of living in a culture of complaint, rather than of gratitude. As acclaimed film producer and director Louie Schwartzberg reminds us in his sweet and uplifting short film *Gratitude,* it can be found in the everyday, in every moment.

One of the best ways to find contentment is by feeling and expressing gratitude. Just think of one thing, however tiny, that one is grateful for. It can be the simplest thing—this breath, that beautiful flower, the smile given by a stranger, a friend, a meal—and then share it.

"Thank you!" is perhaps the most useful and powerful expression of gratitude to learn, in any language. In English, the phrase has a lengthy history rooted in many different cultures. While some aspects remain unclear due to the passage of time and blending of societies, the word *thank* is a derivative of the Old English *thanc,* which means "thought." It was a sentiment that essentially meant those who were grateful would think highly of the person to whom they were grateful. Similarly, the Romance languages, Italian *grazie* and Spanish *gracias* evolved from the Latin phrase *gratias agere,* which essentially means "I give praises."

In any language in which one is fluent, the power of those words is multiplied by the specificity of what follows, for example, "Thank you for sharing your time with me today to teach me how to make berry compote." The accurate labeling of our gratitude enables the recipient to understand what is being appreciated, and to maybe repeat that action again in the future.

—m—

Gratitude comes more easily when we are comfortable and things are going smoothly. Gratitude for our tests and difficulties requires higher consciousness. As noted in chapter 6, Job fell to his knees and gave praise and gratitude to God, despite losing all ten of his children and his entire worldly wealth in one day. During Haydn's journey, I think it is fair to say that the closer he got to his passing— which was the very time he was his most physically challenged—the more gratitude he showed, whether for simply bringing him a glass of water or a straw, helping turn him in his bed, or straightening his blanket.

In climbing mountains, especially at higher altitudes, the lack of normal comforts is inevitable, as these would be too difficult and impractical to transport to such altitudes. As one gains altitude, the oxygen thins, and it quickly becomes a luxury to sleep comfortably, use proper toilets, take a full shower, and eat what you please. High altitude mountain climbing is a great workshop for appreciating the little things in life and taking nothing for granted. It is ironic that when we are comfortable, we tend to forget how fortunate we are. As I reflected upon this, I noticed that Haydn became more grateful the more challenging the climb and the closer he came to his summit. That reminded me of his observation that his faith was strongest when things seemed at their bleakest. The same can be said of his gratitude.

—⁂—

From the moment Haydn was diagnosed, he genuinely didn't seem worried and often made jokes to try to help the rest of us feel comfortable. During the last weeks of his life, the tumor growth in his brain caused some disorientation, and Haydn would sometimes say things we couldn't understand or that didn't make much sense to us. Six days before he passed, when he was so weak that he had stopped eating, he surprised us all by asking, "Who wants to play Code Names?" He didn't lose his sense of humor, neither his joy nor his smile.

In a continued exploration of happiness, a smile is a simple gesture yet unexpectedly generous in its impact. Smiling and laughing are known to boost mood and well-being, not only in the person smiling but in those who are smiled at. One smile is all that is needed to improve one's mood, energy, and overall health. It can help a person's day become better. It can create a positive imprint that ripples beyond our immediate surroundings and experiences.

The power of the smile is also used as a strategy in highly stressful situations, such as sports performance. Kenyan marathon runner Eliud Kipchoge invoked a smiling strategy when he became the first person ever to run a marathon distance in less than two hours in 2019. After the race, he said that smiling through the race helped him cope with difficult and strenuous segments of the course. As I understand, Kipchoge wasn't smiling due to confidence, or to camouflage distress, but simply to help him relax and maintain positive energy. The power of a smile helped him write history!

Fascinatingly, the brain does not distinguish between a fake or a real smile, as both release dopamine, endorphins, and serotonin into the bloodstream. These feel-good messengers not only help with mood, they also counter stress by helping the body to relax, lowering heart rate and blood pressure. Endorphins are also natural painkillers. In a Swedish research study, subjects were shown images of different emotions, including anger, fear, joy, and surprise. They were instructed by the researchers to frown when shown a smiling person. Instead, the participants echoed the smiles in their own expressions, rather than frowning as instructed. Smiling is good for us. And invigorating!

In those sacred and precious hours following Haydn's passing, our family had the privilege to wash his body before wrapping it in silk and placing it in the maple coffin that the funeral home delivered to our house. Even as Karyn gently wiped Haydn's face with rose water, his lips were in enough of an upturn that he was more smiling than frowning, which is rather unusual given the normal relaxation of the facial muscles immediately after death and before the rigor mortis that often gives the face the appearance of a grimace. If dreams are any indication of the state of someone's spirit, then consistently from the many dreams we continued to hear recounted in the weeks and months following Haydn's passing, he still hasn't stopped smiling!

A smile shares hope, spreads affection, and delivers peace. That simple gesture has the power to turn on the light in the dark, to deliver a wave of positivity, to reduce stress in daily life, and to bring greater happiness into the world.

—⁓—

Interestingly, the ancient Greeks didn't use the term *happiness* in their philosophy but used the term *eudaimonia*, which translates as "human flourishing" or "blessedness." That feels more like a journey of ascent and less like scurrying down random holes in the pursuit of the elusive white rabbit of happiness. Human flourishing is also a journey of joy that is revealed from within as much as it is inspired by the terrain we traverse. Chasing rabbits is a search for something outside of ourselves rather than finding the treasure from within. If we catch the rabbit, will we hold happiness in our hearts?

If happiness comes from success, how is success then defined? Shall we join innumerable others who have searched for the ideal job, the perfect partner, the most beautiful apartment, more followers on Instagram, more likes on TikTok . . . but without being any happier once having achieved these? These are all conditional clauses, rooted in the shifty outside world, all proven time and time again not to be guarantees of sustained happiness or contentment. On this, scientific evidence and ancient spiritual teachings are aligned, to remind us that chasing happiness actually makes people unhappy.

> *Unhappiness comes from longing for the things of this world.*
> *Suffering is attachment, grasping, desiring. The secret to*
> *happiness is nonattachment.*
> —Siddhartha Gautama Buddha

So, after all this, why happiness? What about joy, or contentment, or even serenity? In this book, these human qualities are used almost interchangeably. To strive to elevate the word *happiness*, I chose it for this chapter, accepting the risk that happiness is often defined as a state of comfort and ease, with feeling good in the moment, rather than a more long-lasting, connected experience of meaning, of belonging to and serving something beyond oneself. In the wise words of Bengali poet and Nobel Prize winner Rabindranath Tagore:

I slept and dreamt that life was joy. I awoke and saw that life was service. I acted and behold, service was joy.[4]

I cannot overemphasize that feelings of happiness or joy, sadness, or being of service, come from our actions, and those in turn are led by the mind. In verse 2 of *The Dhammapada*, Buddha said, "Our actions are all led by the mind; mind is their master, mind is their maker. If one acts or speaks with a pure state of mind then happiness follows like a shadow that trails constantly behind."

Happiness is generated by "a pure state of mind," meaning a mind that is free from the control of the ego or insistent self. Hence the importance of cultivating selflessness, which is most effectively achieved through service to others. In this lifelong journey, which Haydn pursued to his dying breath, there are no shortcuts, no magic helicopters to take us to the summits of our mountains. There are valuable tools and habits, however, that can lift us up, often when most needed, and increase our happiness. The practices of gratitude, smiling, and detachment ("non-attachment") are achievable by all of us and can cultivate lives filled joy.

This pattern can become habit through conscious effort, little by little, day by day. As verse 118 of *The Dhammapada* goes, "If a man does good, let him do it again and again and let him take delight in it; the accumulation of good causes happiness."

the summit

The more we search for ourselves, the less likely we are to find ourselves; and the more we search for God, and to serve our fellow-men, the more profoundly will we become acquainted with ourselves, and the more inwardly assured. This is one of the great spiritual laws of life.

—SHOGHI EFFENDI, *Lights of Guidance*, 4.391.1

The reason why River and Sea can be
The rulers of the hundred valleys
Is because they adopt the lower position.

—TAO TE CHING, LXVI

They are forever free who renounce all selfish desires and break away from the ego-cage of "I," "me," and "mine" to be united with the Lord. Attain to this, and pass from death to immortality.

—BHAGAVAD GITA 2.71

14.

SELFLESSNESS

"Take the 'self' out of 'self-help'!"

━━━━━━━━━━━━━━━

WHEN HAYDN WAS TWELVE YEARS OLD, KARYN WAS DRIVING WITH our four children in the car when Sian, unprompted, asked her siblings how they would wish to die if they could choose. At Haydn's turn, he said, "I would like to die saving somebody's life."

This reminded Karyn and me of a time when Haydn was just six years old, during a family holiday by the beach in Sanya, on China's Hainan Island. A dear friend of ours, Paul, whom the children knew and loved, had stage 4 cancer and was in the palliative stage of his own journey. We went down to a quiet spot by the beach to sit and say prayers for Paul and his family. Afterward, Haydn held Karyn's hand while walking back to the hotel. He quietly turned to her and said, "Mummy, I hope it's okay, but when we were praying, I asked God to give Uncle Paul my health and to give me Uncle Paul's cancer." About a week later, we received the sad news that Paul had passed away. Karyn and I never forgot this extraordinary selflessness on the part of our precious Haydn.

Putting others before oneself is a quality that Haydn developed from an early age. His journey through suffering from cancer put this and all qualities to the test, as hardships so often do. Around midafternoon on September 23, we received a call from Haydn's oncologist to inform us that Haydn's hemoglobin level was 50 and his platelet count was at 6 (normal levels for men are 135–175 and 150–450 respectively). I instantly knew those numbers were way too low, but the very next sentence snapped me into action. "Please take Haydn to the ER as soon as possible so he can get the transfusions he needs!" We didn't waste any time, and this ER experience, while crowded, turned out to be much more efficient than the previous one. By midnight we were back in the apartment, and the next day I wrote the following in our email update:

> Once the blood transfusion started, a porter appeared and said he was going to move Haydn outside to the corridor so the room could be used for someone else. He kindly took me to show me the spot in the corridor, which was right under a bright fluorescent light, in front of the toilet and beside the door to the soiled utility room. In a very busy and crowded ER, there were plenty of other patients on stretchers along the corridors . . . these patients included all kinds of folk, from accident victims to people just coughing and sneezing with the first signs of winter. The corridor was noisy and very brightly lit, compared to the rather quiet and subdued private space where Haydn was able to rest as he received his much-needed transfusion. The charge nurse came by and asked me to confirm that this move was acceptable, as Haydn was already hooked up and getting his transfusion, so he really didn't need much nursing or medical care and would be discharged as soon as the transfusion was over. From the look on my face (and a closer look at my tear ducts) it was clear that I didn't know how to respond. So, I said I would go back and share the update with Karyn and Haydn. Haydn's response was that if there were more acute-care needs among other patients, then they should get the room, and he would be fine in the corridor.

Blood transfusions are a reminder of the uniquely human act of donating blood purely for the sake of helping others who need it. That the donor rarely knows the recipient makes this an act of unquestionable altruism. Being a recipient of a bag of platelets, likely from four donors, is awe inspiring. To receive such life-saving gifts from complete strangers is a testament to the beauty of humanity and to the goodness of folk who, the world over, give for one another, whether they donate their time, material wealth, or their own blood. Each time Haydn received a transfusion—and there were twenty of those in all—he would say a prayer of gratitude, praying that, whoever the donor may be, that selfless soul might receive bounties and blessings.

Accompanying Haydn through the hours of a transfusion, whether of blood or platelets, was not particularly eventful unless there was a reaction that needed medical intervention. Nonetheless, it was a profound, soul-stirring experience. The material reality of what was happening was clear. There was magic to watching a pale and rather gaunt lad with dangerously low hemoglobin gradually return to some color and feel stronger. The spiritual reality of watching a life being saved was equally clear and often evoked a profound sense of awe and respect. It was not unusual to sit beside Haydn's bed on those occasions and experience tears of hope and joy. Here we were witnessing cooperation, mutual aid, and reciprocity that reignited hope and trust in the goodness and oneness of humanity.

Humans sometimes go to extraordinary lengths to help others, even at our own cost. Psychology researcher Abigail Marsh studies the human capacity for altruism, the act of helping others with no apparent benefit to oneself. In the department of psychology and the interdisciplinary neuroscience program at Georgetown University, Marsh focuses on social and affective neuroscience. She addresses questions using multiple approaches that include functional and structural brain imaging in adolescents and adults from both typical and nontypical populations, as well as behavioral, cognitive, genetic, and pharmacological techniques. While Marsh recognizes that compassion is a key driver of altruism, her research indicates that "the brains of highly altruistic people are different in fundamental ways."[1]

Marsh's research uses brain imaging studies to demonstrate that the size of the amygdala, that part of the brain that recognizes fearful expressions, is about 20% smaller than average among psychopaths and children/adolescents with severe conduct problems and limited empathy. In contrast, the amygdalas of altruistic people—kidney donors being the subjects used in Marsh's research—are about 8% larger than average. Marsh is convinced that "the roots of altruism and compassion are just as much a part of human nature as cruelty and violence, maybe even more so."[2] As we begin to understand which parts of the brain are associated with acts of altruism, or their opposite in acts of selfishness or cruelty to others, it may be that science begins to contribute to our understanding and fostering of selflessness.

In 1956, British historian Arnold Toynbee published *An Historian's Approach to Religion*. Toynbee notes that one can distill a common faith experience, described as the "spiritual presence," from the diversity of beliefs and practices across all religions. It is the transforming influence of this "presence" in these religions that leads to an "act of self-sacrifice"—the process of "giving up self-centeredness" and focusing one's life on a new center: the Absolute Reality and spiritual presence behind these religions. Service to that Absolute Reality, or God, is expressed in all the higher religions through selfless service to His creatures.

Today the nations of the world are self-engaged, occupied with mortal and transitory accomplishments, consumed by the fires of passion and self. Self is dominant; enmity and animosity prevail. Nations and peoples are thinking only of their worldly interests and outcomes.

> *You must deal with all in loving-kindness in order that this precious seed entrusted to your planting may continue to grow and bring forth its perfect fruit. The love and mercy of God will accomplish this through you if you have love in your own heart.*
> —'ABDU'L-BAHÁ,
> *The Promulgation of Universal Peace, 3.7*

During the eight months of Haydn's seemingly endless hospital and clinic visits, not once did he ever go before Karyn into or out of the elevator. He always let his mother go first, even when he was so frail and weak that he sometimes found it hard to stand or walk beyond a few steps. It is an extraordinary quality to think of others and how they feel in such moments. Haydn's consideration for others, beyond our own family, was consistent until the very end. When there were visitors, Haydn made sure they were taken care of, whether being offered a seat or a cup of tea. When he was so weak he could no longer move from his bed, he remained attentive to our sleep. He wanted to know we were taking care of ourselves.

One of Haydn's friends, Angus, wrote to our family the day after Haydn's passing. Here are some excerpts from his letter:

> *I am so sorry for your loss. Haydn was the kindest, wittiest, and most spirited person I have ever known. He was the finest chap at Wellington and made our sixth form incredibly special.*
>
> *We were not the most functional year group before Haydn arrived and I would not have envied him entering Benson at that point. Despite this he fitted in brilliantly and changed us into better people. . . . He has had a lasting impact on all of us and I am so grateful that I was able to spend time with him.*
>
> *He was so supportive and selfless during stressful times. The brutal essay editing and untold hours of flashcard testing, while exhausting, helped me so much, and I know that it was his generosity and friendliness that got us to the end of it. Through the challenges and triumphs of those two years he was always present and supportive. He was incredibly bright and so humble about it. He would show me the sketches from his portfolio, which were truly stunning. I would have loved to see those buildings in real life. We also had a fantastic time visiting Cambridge, eating poutine, imagining ourselves there, and then not getting in. Haydn still had us smiling by the evening. He was a shoulder to lean on, a true listener, and the best person to ground you. He also had the sharpest sense of humor which could take you by surprise and leave you giggling all evening.*
>
> *He was so involved in everything we did. He would save our poorly*

planned, last-minute house art efforts, and was formidable on the basketball court or in goal. Long summer evenings kicking a football around with Haydn will be enduring memories. He was the best presence and the loveliest chap to spend day-to-day life with. He was interested and interesting. He was selfless and altruistic.

It is impossible to sum up the lasting influence he has had on me, and I have enjoyed sharing time with him so much. I am thankful for everything that he has done.

—⚬—

We are born into this world fully dependent on others to feed us, wash us, clothe us, indeed to take care of all of our needs. Gradually we learn to be independent. Fortunately, the journey of growth is designed to take us beyond independence to interdependence. There lies our greatest strength, whether as individuals or as a society. In the world of nature, there is really no such thing as true independence. Everything is connected to everything else, whether at the microscopic or macroscopic level. There is no greater teacher or classroom than that of Mother Nature if we wish to learn interdependence, cooperation, and reciprocity. And in nature, there is no more sophisticated and complex organism or operating system than the human body. If we doubt the power of unity, we need only look inside ourselves to see the work of genius, or Genius.

We could say that the newborn baby, pure and undefiled by life's tests and the inevitable mistakes we all make, is still 100% selfish. To the newborn babe, they are at the center of the universe, attended to in every detail and need of their life. Hopefully, by the time we leave this life, we have moved on from being 100% selfish to 100% selfless. That would make us saints; yet we can at least try to journey in that direction. The world's major religious teachings describe the journey of spiritual growth as being the journey of dying to the self, abandoning the insistent self, letting go of the ego. Religious traditions also describe the purity of the newborn babe and call us to maintain this purity in our adult lives. As Christ taught, in Matthew 18:3, "Be like unto children if you wish to enter the kingdom of heaven." The difference is that the purity of the newborn is based upon weakness, whereas the purity of the wise person who has developed a pure and gentle heart is based upon strength and compassion, often forged through the trials and tribulations of life.

Before Haydn's cancer, I thought often about the journey of life being from selfishness to selflessness. I saw a logic and beauty in understanding the human journey as one moving from dependence to independence to interdependence. I had not yet reflected much upon the unexpected return to dependence that occurs in illness or old-age fragility. At the very end of his life, Haydn was nineteen years old and his illness necessitated a premature, gradual return to support with such basics as eating, washing, being turned in his bed, and so on. What was the lesson in this? I think it is to maintain an authentic respect for the mountaineer and pivot without hesitation to support the unique challenges faced during their climb.

Continuing the metaphor, one can imagine climbing Everest— whether during the ascent or descent—where every member commits to attaining the summit. Every member pours in countless hours of training and leaves behind loved ones and home comforts for several months. Every member experiences some levels of discomfort to serve the team, to touch the top and return again. Then, suddenly and unexpectantly, one member requires immediate support to descend quickly due to injury or illness. The work, the challenge, the acute attention now more than ever belongs to the team's lead, who is likely most familiar with the route and how the body responds in such situations. The degree of mindfulness, detachment, and selflessness required has now increased significantly, and quickly. Many great mountain guides have experienced rescue missions to save the lives, or a life, of those who become most challenged by the mountain. Imagine selecting a guide for a formidable climb ahead. Would anyone ever choose to place one's life in the hands of someone who was only a fair-weather guide?

—⁂—

In terms of parables to illustrate selflessness, the allegory of the long spoons is surely one of the most loved and oft retold. It is attributed to several sources, including Rabbi Haim of Romshishok, Lithuania, who apparently told this story to his congregation:

I wanted to know the difference between Heaven and Hell, so I decided to visit them both.

I first went to Hell. There I found people sitting at long tables filled with sumptuous food, but they were all emaciated and starving. They had spoons that were six feet long and could not bend their arms in such a way to feed themselves. Both arms were splinted with wooden slats so the people could not bend either elbow to bring the food to their mouths.

I then went to Heaven and saw a slightly different situation. The people there were also sitting around long tables piled with food. They, too, had six-foot-long spoons, but they were all well nourished and happy because they were feeding each other across the table.

I then understood. Heaven and Hell offer the same circumstances and conditions. The critical difference is in the way people treat each other and care for others more than just thinking of themselves.

The long spoons allegory has become part of the folklore across several religions and cultures. For example, Judaism, Hinduism, Buddhism, and Christianity all have similar teachings. In medieval Europe, the food in the story is a bowl of stew; in China, it is a bowl of rice being eaten with long chopsticks. In whichever form, it exemplifies that selflessness, as a tool in overall wellness, expands spiritual fulfilment as the gains of giving are immeasurable and often create a powerful ripple effect.

In chapter 1, I shared that Haydn's notes included the title for something he intended to write: *Why the Self in Self-help Is Unimportant*. Although this book is a tribute of sorts to Haydn, this chapter is especially so. I dearly wish it was he who might have written it, and in several ways he did, for the story is his, which he wrote through his life.

> *Every imperfect soul is self-centered and thinketh only of his own good. But as his thoughts expand a little he will begin to think of the welfare and comfort of his family. If his ideas still more widen, his concern will be the felicity of his fellow citizens; and if still they widen, he will be thinking of the glory of his land and of his race. But when ideas and views reach the utmost degree of expansion and attain the stage of perfection, then will he be interested in the exaltation of humankind. He will then be the well-wisher of all men and the seeker of the weal and prosperity of all lands. This is indicative of perfection.*
> —'ABDU'L-BAHÁ,
> *Selections from the Writings of 'Abdu'l-Bahá*

*When the Buddha was asked, "Sir, what do you and your monks practice?" he replied, "We sit, we walk, and we eat." The questioner continued, "But sir, everyone sits, walks, and eats," and the Buddha told him, "When we sit, we **know** we are sitting. When we walk, we **know** we are walking. When we eat, we **know** we are eating."*

—THICH NHAT HANH, *Living Buddha, Living Christ*

The Blessed One (Buddha) said, "Mindfulness of death, when developed and pursued, is of great fruit and great benefit. It plunges into the Deathless, has the Deathless as its final end. Therefore, you should develop mindfulness of death."

—*Sutra Collection (M, Part-2), 14.3*

A high-minded self-awareness and a consistent seriousness with no forfeit of dignity are necessary if a man wants to be of service to others. He who throws himself away in order to do the bidding of a superior diminishes his own position without thereby giving lasting benefit to the other.

—I CHING, 41.15

15.

MINDFULNESS

"To live our lives as if it really mattered . . ."

IN THE LAST WEEK OF HIS LIFE, HAYDN SEEMED TO START HIS MOVE toward the next world. The veil between this life and the next seemed to be pulling back to give him a glimpse of the next adventure that awaited him. Occasionally, Haydn would say things that seemed to be more about communicating with his new associates on the other side of the veil than with those of us he would be leaving on this side. On May 17, two days before he passed away, Haydn pointed into the air with a shaking hand and asked Karyn in a whisper, "Is that your family?" Karyn's answer was brilliant; simply, "It could be!" A few days prior, he was speaking on the phone with one of his closest friends, and she was sharing with him the various decisions she had to make involving her work. Haydn paused and said groggily, "I have only one decision to make."

In 1881, T. W. Rhys Davids coined the term *mindfulness* from the original texts of the Buddhist teachings, the Satipaṭṭhāna Sutta. The word *Sati*, that was used to teach the Buddhist "present-moment-awareness" became "mindfulness." As such, it was subsequently adopted in the context of Western clinical psychology in the 1990s, notably in the work of Jon Kabat-Zinn, PhD. Kabat-Zinn's founding of the mindfulness-based stress reduction program at the University of Massachusetts Medical Center paved the way for mindfulness being incorporated into behavioral medicine and then in turn aided the development of mindfulness-based cognitive therapy. Knowledge that was born from Eastern wisdom and practices from twenty-six hundred years ago was put to scientific tests and through thousands of clinical studies by Western clinical psychology, neuropsychology, and neuroscience. Kabat-Zinn explains mindfulness best, in his book *Full Catastrophe Living*:

> *Mindfulness is not merely a concept or a good idea. It is a way of being. And its synonym, awareness, is a kind of knowing that is simply bigger than thought and gives us many more options for how we might choose to be in relationship to whatever arises in our minds and hearts, our bodies and our lives. . . . The practice of mindfulness involves finding, recognizing, and making use of that in us which is already okay, already beautiful, already whole by virtue of our being human— and drawing upon it to live our lives as if it really mattered how we stand in relationship to what arises, whatever it is.*

Although Haydn went to a school that prided itself on being one of the first schools in the UK to teach mindfulness, he rarely mentioned the word. Instead, he simply lived mindfully. In so many aspects of his life, whether in the simple habits of eating or brushing one's teeth, or in the subtle relationships with family and friends, or complete strangers, Haydn was engaged mindfully. Here was a nineteen-year-old young man who famously took two hours to pick flowers in the gardens of the Chile Bahá'í house of worship as a gift for his mother before leaving his volunteer service. Mindful gift giving exemplified!

There are many, many expressions of mindfulness found in the everyday. One way to practice mindfulness is to makes one's bed at the start of each day, a habit of Haydn's since early childhood. For the impressive impact of this practice, I recommend listening to the inspiring commencement speech "Make Your Bed" by US Navy admiral William H. McRaven, in which he states so clearly:

If you make your bed every morning you will have accomplished the first task of the day. It will give you a small sense of pride, and it will encourage you to do another task and another and another. By the end of the day, that one task completed will have turned into many tasks completed. Making your bed will also reinforce the fact that little things in life matter. If you can't do the little things right, you will never do the big things right. And, if by chance you have a miserable day, you will come home to a bed that is made—that you made—and a made bed gives you encouragement that tomorrow will be better.

Mindful eating is another expression of mindfulness. Haydn was a slow eater. This made it hard for him at boarding school, when peers would gulp down their food and be off, leaving him only half-way through his meal. One night, Haydn shared that he really appreciated those times when a friend would stay with him, patiently waiting for him to finish his meal, rather than leaving him alone at the table. We all know that eating in a slow manner is better for digestion, but did you know that Buddhist monks are supposed to chew each morsel of food thirty times as part of their discipline of mindful eating? In so doing, they give their full attention to the food, appreciating it and becoming one with the source of nourishment.

Mountain climbing demands full concentration. Mindful climbing, however, is more likely achieved by a seasoned mountaineer who has become routine, orderly, and systematic and can therefore absorb the striking surroundings. Add serenity to such qualities, and, yes, it was a gift to this climb that Haydn had all of these. He always started his day by making his bed and kept his room tidy. In the two years Haydn was at boarding school in England, he would often come home on the weekends, not just for some home cooking but also to get his laundry done. He would arrive at home with his dirty laundry . . . folded. Haydn's artwork was a lesson in precision, and he had to push himself to loosen up and let his heart, and his charcoal pencil or his paintbrush, dance freely. By the time he graduated, he had learned to be freer and more confident in the ways he did things and was able to make fun of himself for being so orderly. He strove for excellence in all that he set out to do, and his organizational skills helped him to plan the work and work the plan. These habits of awareness unwittingly helped prepare him for the mountain climb of his life.

Such practices of mindfulness don't mean one doesn't relax and chill. Quite the contrary. One of Haydn's favorite words was *chill*, and he savored the idea of chilling with friends in Sri Lanka or being by the beach and just chilling. When he was informed by the oncologists in Toronto that his disease had spread and that the curative journey had ended, we drove home and sat on the bed, and he started to tell us what he envisioned for his funeral. I remember he said he wanted it to have a "chill vibe." This might not be the tone or language we normally expect of funerals. But Haydn was clear that his funeral was not to be a sad occasion, though it would, of course, be dignified. He knew we would be grieving, but he insisted that no one wear black. He said that twice. He wanted the focus to be mindfully centered on savoring and celebrating the wonderful life he had lived. In fact, he was quite specific about his funeral being a time to be grateful and joyful, with the arrangements to have a lightness of touch, to be fresh and relaxed.

So, while one can eat mindfully and live mindfully, one can also die mindfully. Both Eastern and Western traditions have explicit teachings that guide the dying to a conscious and graceful death without fear or shame. There is a body of medieval Christian literature called *Ars Moriendi*, or *Art of Dying*, that provided guidance for the dying and those who attended them. In the West, this wisdom was lost in the late eighteenth century during the rush to industrialization and modernity. For most of the twentieth century, death was almost completely denied in the West, with the dying patient told "you're really looking better today" and family members counseled to avoid mentioning the word. By the late sixties, things began to change. In 1967 the first modern hospice was founded in London, and in 1969 Elizabeth Kubler-Ross published *On Death and Dying*, her research into the grieving process.

On March 19, a few days before we left New York to return to Ottawa for our last weeks with Haydn, a dear friend introduced us to Dr. Shamim, one of the most kind and brilliant family doctors I have met, who also worked in palliative care in the community. In a phone call with him before our arrival in Ottawa, he said that he would be honored to be Haydn's palliative care doctor and shared that death need not be a negative or awful experience. On the contrary, he assured us that with the right kind of environment and family support, and with medications for pain management, dying could be a positive experience for Haydn and for the family. We knew we had found the right doctor, and we started planning for how to be at home together with Haydn in whatever time remained. Home hospice felt right for us all, even though we knew it could be challenging, so we researched our local palliative care resources, including backup hospice beds if we couldn't manage.

One of the reasons that mindful dying may appear a far cry from the reality of our modern, frenetic, urbanized life is that much of modern society, irrespective of geography, has developed a culture in which the mortal body is idolized. This sets us up for disillusionment and a crisis when hopes are dashed on the rocks of reality. Until we shatter the idol of the mortal body, death will continue to be the worst thing, likely the most frightening thing, that could ever happen to us. If we need a more useful focus for our aspirations, it might be healthier to consider our immortality—that our spiritual reality, our soul, is eternal and has been set by a loving creator on a path of eternal growth and learning. Haydn saw that path as one of that of a lover moving toward his beloved. He prayed that he would be mindful and faithful to the end, and sure footed as he made the transition from this life to the more abundant life of what lay beyond. On such a journey, through all the worlds of God, the physical death of the mortal body is just one of several milestones, just as we each passed a milestone when we left behind the world of the womb and entered this physical world to continue our growth and development here.

With such a perspective, one realizes that conscious dying is really part of conscious living. Indeed, it is an essential part, and there is wisdom in reflecting on the afterlife. Ironically, such a practice actually helps us to make wiser choices in this life, and with those wiser choices comes more happiness.

When Haydn began his palliative care and prepared to transition from this world, his preschool teacher, Jessica, shared that *phowa* is a Vajrayana Buddhist meditation practice. It may be described as "the practice of conscious dying." This is a letter she wrote to us, almost three months after Haydn's passing:

> *One thing I wanted to mention about conscious dying and your observation of its indicator of mindfulness is that I recall Haydn having a very steady, concentrated ability from a young age. He is the only two-to-three-year-old who would regularly work with a material for over two hours at a time without interruption. I never saw this in any other child that age. Of course, mindfulness is more than concentration, but it is a big factor of being able to be present in each moment to moment "as-it-is." How incredible that Haydn has inspired us all in his dying.*
>
> *I also wanted to mention [that] one of the first Buddhist teachings I ever received as a teenager myself was studying some Pali, the ancient language of Buddha Shakyamuni. Pali is a derivative of Sanskrit, and the Buddha chose to teach in Pali because it was the local language, the language of the people (as opposed to teaching in a more academic dialect). I learnt that the Pali word for death, when taught by the Buddha was always conjoined with the word for life, or rebirth. The essence is that the Buddha always taught "death-birth," or jati-marana. So, death was never a singular event of finality. That death is birth (or rebirth) is, I think, a shared teaching in many religions. This is something I was reminded of in my dreams of Haydn before he died. Because of the open, light, beatific quality of his being, I felt his passing*

as a birthing. And as I recall in the Bahá'í teachings that death is the entrance to the Almighty is indeed a birth. While my heart grieves the earthly loss of Haydn's presence, I do feel an incredible peace in the way his passing was supported—consciously by your family. It is so rare! And in this way, I am in awe of both of you for your strength to support the opening of his birthing "as-it-is" when that moment naturally occurred.

In the days leading up to Haydn's passing, there was nothing more surreal than planning the practicalities of his end-of-life arrangements. While most parents were helping their teens choose bedding for university dorm rooms, Karyn was choosing a casket, designing a memorial program, and ironing clothes for the funeral, all while Haydn chatted quietly or rested in the next room. In between hours of sleep, we tried to consider his every need and mindfully tend to those needs with love, beauty, and nobility. We brought him into this world with those intentions, and we were determined to accompany him to the veil with the same.

One week before Haydn passed, we gathered around his bedside for our normal evening prayers. Haydn's voice had become so soft in the previous couple of days that it was harder to hear him. But that evening he dug deep and powerfully joined us as we sang an Arabic phrase—"Allah'u'Abha!"—which translates to "God is the All-Glorious." This is also referred to in the Bahá'í Faith as the Greatest Name and is a prayer in itself. The melody adds to the beauty of this chant, which Haydn loved since childhood. This was the first word that was said into his ears when he exited the womb world and entered this earthly world. It was also the song we sang as we carried his coffin out of the house a week later, and again when we carried it from the hearse to his final resting place in Wakefield, Canada.

The next day, Karyn suggested that we sing "Allah'u'Abha!" again and Haydn nodded. He sang with us, frail, but finding his voice with what reserves he had. Each time we thought we'd come to the end, he started up again. We glanced around the room at one another, and in unspoken agreement we let him carry us along until he was ready to stop. The beauty and poignancy of that moment lingered in the room as we sat reverently to savor it. Keyan broke the silence with a song that we used to sing with the children when they were much younger. The refrain is "Strive that your actions, day by day, may be beautiful prayers." We were tired and struggled to remember the words that followed. The tune sounded awful and Karyn whispered, "At least we tried!" Haydn raised his eyebrows as if to say, "Hmm . . . but still so far off the mark," which made us all laugh.

Four days before he passed, Haydn was in bed and in quite some pain. Although the medication helped manage Haydn's discomfort, there were times when he experienced breakthrough levels that tested the limit of what he was able to endure. His body was afflicted with the combination of cancer spreading in his spinal cord, affecting his nerves, and the side effects of multiple medications, which included urinary retention. As one of the doctors shared with us, it was as if there were a fire in the control room. That evening, Haydn tried to get up to pee, his weakened legs hung over the edge of the bed, his emaciated frame was a shadow of his athletic form just nine months earlier, and he began wailing in pain. Haydn turned to Karyn and asked, now at the very close of his earthly life, "What time is the flight?" To which, Karyn wisely replied, "Anytime you want."

Haydn's pain spilled over into the following day. Exasperated, he turned again to Karyn and asked, somewhat agitated and maybe at the end of whatever still tethered him to this world, "Why can't I die?" It was really the final push to the summit, and he was almost begging. It had been a grueling and long journey. Karyn ever so lovingly replied, "When you are ready, you'll go." To which Haydn replied, "Where should I go?" In that moment, Karyn didn't want to tell him where he should go. Such sacred choices should not be dictated by others, so she tenderly replied, "Anywhere you want."

For our purposes here, we will use "mindfulness," "awareness," "being in presence," or "living in the now" relatively interchangeably. My personal preference is "awareness" because I find it less loaded. I also find it helpful to visualize the path of life being a journey of raising awareness, as part of raising consciousness, both in being and doing, both within ourselves as individuals and within our societies. Starting with being more aware of our words, we will naturally begin to raise the level of our conversations. Through meaningful and nourishing conversations, we seed the ground of culture. Through nurturing culture, we may eventually raise the level of consciousness. These are the deepest and most profound processes that have led to the birth and growth of civilizations. This is the big picture of our journey, as individuals and as a society.

In mindfulness, one nourishes the experience of simply being aware of our thoughts, letting them be, observing them without attachment or judgment, without holding onto them or letting them hold onto us. In using meditation to cultivate mindfulness, one allows the thoughts of the mind to pass by, through locating our awareness in a deeper-seated place such as through focus on breathing, particularly belly breathing, which is helpful in getting our awareness out of our heads and closer to our center of gravity.

In Chinese, the Taoist principle of *Wu-wei*, is often translated as "nondoing" or "nonaction." But this not the same as doing nothing, in fact quite the opposite. To practice *Wu-wei* is to "go with the flow" and requires great awareness, mindfulness, and being responsive to the moment and all that it holds. It is like using our thoughts to switch off our thoughts. The Taoist principle of *Wu-wei*, taught by Lao Tzu in the Tao Te Ching, has similarities to the spiritual teachings of detachment and the nonclinging to individual ego in favor of being in tune and acting through the influence of our inherent divine nature.

With all the talk of mindfulness and fully living in the present moment, the difficult question is how we can live in the present moment when things are not the way we want or expect them to be. When we say, "Really, I didn't sign up for this!" Some opportunities come only once in a while, perhaps once a year, once every few years, or perhaps once in a lifetime. Those are the ones we really can't afford to miss. All opportunities come only at their moment, and that is where we need to stand to capture them. If our thoughts are stuck in the past or overly focused on the future, then we set our-selves up for disappointment and missing our moment. It really doesn't matter how good or bad things are in the present. It is more helpful to see things as they are rather than waste time in judgment that cannot change the present moment.

All of the past culminates in where we stand right now, to such an extent that if any of the millions and trillions of past events were not the way they were, this would not be the now we live in. Being in the now is to be at the meeting point of both the past and the future. Indeed, it's the entirety of the past and the entirety of the future. We are all where we need to be, right here, right now. How beautiful that it is called the present! And how poignant and purposeful life is when we live in mindful presence and receive such presents.

One sign of awareness is to be so present to the moment that we do not attempt to crash multiple moments into one, by multitasking that ends up being a habit of distraction rather than of focus—usu-ally with the result of not achieving excellence in many, or any, of those multiple tasks.

Teenagers are no strangers to multitasking. Increasing research shows the habit of multitasking to be less effective than we might imagine and even detrimental to mindful living. Watching Haydn live his days was like watching a mountaineer work his mountain. There were times when a lot was going on, but he didn't seem to be overwhelmed or distracted, nor did he seem to be shuffling back and forth with a lot of tasks, none of which would have been done very well given our context. For sure, there was complexity and simultaneity beyond anything that could be managed with lists and singular tasks that could be ticked off as they were completed. This being said, there is an important distinction between multitasking and parallel processing. Imagine fixing bolts into the rock face as one scales it, working with the rope, quick draws and other gear, coordinating with the climb team, heeding changing weather conditions, dealing with the need for food and rest, going to the toilet, and any number of other factors. Climbers don't usually take Post-it notes to write down or review what follows what. They don't separate and dichotomize the tasks but rather see them all as part of a singular story, a singular challenge, a singular reality, in which all parts of the puzzle are constituents of one coherent and coordinated whole. In the moment to moment of the climb, all parts belong in the singular process. Of course, some elements of the puzzle move into the foreground, then recede into the background. They are all always in the picture and simply fluctuate in and out of focus depending on the now.

With an increasing attention being paid to the power of now, there is a risk that some might imagine that this is a call to live *for* the present moment. That can translate to being very hedonistic, paying attention only to short-term thinking and short-term solutions. My hope is to live not *for* the present moment but *in* the present moment, so to live *for* the future. One day, some weeks after Haydn's passing, Keyan turned to us and casually said, "If you don't have a goal, the present means nothing." Karyn and I stopped and looked at each other, smiling. Those are wise words indeed.

Blessed are all they that put their trust in Him.

—THE BOOK OF PSALMS, TEHILIM, 2:12

O my God, Thy Trust hath been returned unto Thee.

—BAHÁ'U'LLÁH, BAHÁ'Í PRAYERS, 9.23

Verily we are God's, and to Him shall we return.

—THE KORAN 2:156

16.

TRUST

"We have each been entrusted to a family,
who will one day return that Trust."

EXHAUSTED AND HIGHLY MEDICATED FOR PAIN, NO LONGER EATING
or drinking, Haydn turned to Karyn and said, "Mum, I'm not sure
what to do." He consulted her about everything, but this one she
knew he had to do himself—he was on his own to trust and surrender his will to the Will of God. There is no agenda or script for such
a time in life. Conscious dying is not passive. It takes every ounce of
one's inner resilience and fortitude to trust in the journey. Like a
high-altitude mountaineer within striking distance of the summit
but truly spent and managing on very little oxygen, one is inching
forward by willpower, resilience, and the grace of God.

The first thing that Haydn asked for when he heard the doctors'
prognosis on January 10 was to be together with family. This was the
climb team who would accompany him on his final push to the summit. Around this time, Karyn shared, "We have each been entrusted
to a family, who will one day return that Trust." I found this deeply
comforting, a clarion insight that was like a rope, binding us together, far beyond being physically together in the same space. Karyn
and I believed that our children were given to us as trusts from God.
They don't belong to us, any more than we belong to them. If we see
our children as trusts from God, and raise them so, then it should

make no difference whether they are biological or adopted. Our role as parents is to be guardians of those trusts, to guide, love, and protect them, until such time as we, or they, return to the source of all sacred trusts.

Trust is the silent and often underrated companion to love. We usually associate family with love, providing a setting of love that nurtures each family member; however, without trust, love is on unstable ground. Stephen M. R. Covey's popular book *The Speed of Trust* is aptly subtitled *The One Thing That Changes Everything*. This is how Covey introduces his timely insights:

> *There is one thing that is common to every individual, relationship, team, family, organization, nation, economy, and civilization throughout the world—one thing which, if removed, will destroy the most powerful government, the most successful business, the most thriving economy, the most influential leadership, the greatest friendship, the strongest character, the deepest love. On the other hand, if developed and leveraged, that one thing has the potential to create unparalleled success and prosperity in every dimension of life. Yet, it is the least understood, most neglected, and most underestimated possibility of our time. That one thing is trust.*

Much has been written about the power of trust, although less about the concept of trusteeship. When we guard a precious trust, we become trustees. Each of us is a trustee, whether of the children we raise or of the earth that has been passed on to us—its mountains, forests, deserts, seas, and all its living creatures, especially its peoples. Similarly, each one of us is also a trust that has been entrusted, not only to our parents and families but to the human family:

> *Each individual needs to understand that, since the body of humankind is one and indivisible, each member of the human race is born into the world as a trust of the whole and that the advantage of*

the part in a world society is best served by promoting the advantage of the whole.[1]

A few weeks after Haydn passed away, my mother called me. She knew we were grieving and dealing with a truly awful loss. Lovingly, she said, "You know that we, the whole family, lost Haydn." It was a timely, important reminder. Not only the family but Haydn's friends were all feeling the loss, all grieving in different ways and to different degrees. Extending the circle to embrace the human family of which every one of us is a part, the world lost Haydn. In the weeks and months that followed, we received letters and heard stories from people who hardly knew Haydn or even knew him only through others, but who had been moved by some aspect of his life, particularly his suffering with grace and gratitude through cancer.

When we put the boot on the other foot, we also realize that when someone makes their own "hero's journey" through suffering, we too have been part of that journey, whether consciously or not. Every time someone earns a Nobel Prize, wins Olympic or Paralympic gold, or summits whatever their personal mountain of achievement, we each achieve something from that brother or sister whom we may not know but who is clearly part of our collective human family. As the astronaut Neil Armstrong famously said, placing his left foot on the lunar surface, on July 20, 1969: "That's one small step for man, one giant leap for mankind." Because of trusteeship, that we are all trusts of the whole, that was our step too.

Larger companies usually have executive teams to make corporate decisions for the growth and health of the business, but increasingly they also have boards of trustees. Trustees are usually appointed due to their prior experience in business or in positions of responsibility in society. They are the proverbial wise owls whose wisdom can be good for the business without being involved in the running of the business or even having a stake in it. In more profound ways, this is what happens in a family when one realizes that our role as trustees of a precious trust, especially one so sacred as a child, is a position of great honor and responsibility. Our joys and pains of being entrusted to be Haydn's family during such an ordeal as his were also unlike normal joy or pain, as they, too, had a depth and beauty that I can only describe as sacred. Given that we were dealing with a human soul, how could it be otherwise?

Khalil Gibran, the Lebanese American author of *The Prophet*, wrote this oft-quoted verse in his poem *On Children* that so beautifully captures the idea that we are trustees of our children:

> *Your children are not your children.*
> *They are the sons and daughters of Life's longing for itself.*
> *They come through you but not from you,*
> *And though they are with you yet they belong not to you.*

Haydn's final weeks, and certainly his final days with us, were both very worldly—dealing with his body's physical demise—and very otherworldly. We witnessed his spiritual qualities shine, particularly his kindness, gentleness, calmness, caring, and gratitude. On May 14, Haydn asked Karyn, "Can I just be home chilling?" He paused, looked around, and said, "Oh, I am home. I thought I was in the hospital." Karyn replied, "It's wonderful you are home. You can chill here." That day we moved Haydn back to the sitting room, to the adjustable bed. We sat on the edge of the bed, Karyn with her arm around Haydn. As he leaned into her embrace and support, Haydn said, "It's nice to be here."

During those final days, we strained to hear what Haydn was saying; he would sometimes whisper to Karyn, "I love you." It was surreal to be going through this during COVID-19. When family or friends came to visit Haydn, they could not enter the house. Rather, the stream of visitors would come to the window and wave to Haydn, or sign to him, or lift up their dogs to him and bring him some joy. One day, the owner of Haydn's favorite pizza restaurant drove to the house to deliver him a pizza. Haydn sat up in bed, even though he was feeling awful, turned toward the window, put his hand on his heart, bowed his head, and blew her a gentle kiss to thank her. She shared that she felt like a queen in that moment! He made time, gave people his best, even when he was physically not his best. Despite the pain he was in, Haydn wouldn't leave a visitor at the window without a smile, often placing his hand to his heart and bowing to them or, in whatever way he could, showing his gratitude. Despite his fatigue, he was gracious in spirit and generous with his love. Some friends would come and pray on the porch for hours. One family, from the local church, brought a Coleman stove that they set up in the garden to cook a meal for the family and then left it on the doorstep. This outpouring of love did not fall on fallow soil. These gestures of love and support deeply moved Haydn, although in his humility, he wondered what he could possibly have done to deserve them.

Haydn's grandmother, one of the most sincere and devout Christians I have ever met, was determined not to give up hope that Haydn would live through this ordeal. She was convinced that a healing miracle would happen, even at the eleventh hour. Because of COVID protocols, she would sit on our porch, wrapped in a blanket to protect her in the cold. Between her deepest, most ardent prayers, she would look up, watching her beloved grandson through the paned window between the porch and the living room. On May 18, the day before Haydn passed, we begged her to come inside, setting COVID protocols aside at least for this day. She came in and sat beside Haydn, holding his hand. She tenderly kissed him on the forehead and wished him well. Her last words, a final prayer as she stood beside Haydn, uttered through a loving grandmother's tears, "O Lord, Haydn has been a gift to our family, and now we give that gift back to you."

Later that afternoon, Karyn and Haydn looked deeply, for what seemed like forever, into each other's eyes. Karyn smiled to comfort and warm Haydn's heart, while hers was breaking. In those last weeks, they held hands a lot, staring at the lake. Often Haydn broke their silence, saying, "I'm so blessed." At one point on that last afternoon, Haydn was stroking Karyn's hand over and over again as he comforted her. After evening prayers, Haydn slowly but deliberately lifted his hand out from the cashmere blanket that had accompanied him for so much of the journey, and with a small gentle wave, he whispered, "Bye," before adding in a small and almost inaudible whisper, "I love you guys." Those were his last words.

Trust became our own family's security, the guide ropes that held us firmly attached to the mountain that is our faith. We were challenged to accept that the Will of God is not always the same as our own will. Those times are difficult, for sure, yet they require an unwavering trust. In such a moment of acquiescence and awe, one summits one's own mountain, in the freedom of letting go and trusting in a power and wisdom much greater than one's own.

Haydn must have known how tired Karyn and I were. His breathing was labored, and we were up every couple of hours to administer subcutaneous medication to help relieve him. The final nights before his passing, Haydn's siblings agreed to be on three-hour shifts by Haydn's bedside, watching over him. On that last night, Karyn and I managed some sleep but woke to take over from Sian at 6:00 a.m. She shared that Haydn's breathing had started to change pattern.

Haydn's head kept turning toward the right, toward the stone wall. We could see only his profile. Karyn prayed by Haydn's side, comforting him as she kissed his hands and forehead, stroking his chest gently, over and over to bring him peace, saying there was nothing to worry about. She gently whispered, "All is well my love, and all will be well." The room was calm. The sun had risen, and its rays streamed into the room, caressing the white sheets that held our precious Haydn, awaiting his leave. Keyan joined us at 9:00 a.m. and offered to be with his brother while Karyn and I slipped into the kitchen to have a piece of toast and coffee. The coffee machine gurgled gently, much like the sound of Haydn's breathing. Karyn distinctly remembers taking the last sip of her coffee—yes, Haydn was considerate to the very end—when Keyan appeared and said, "Mom and Dad, you might want to come."

We moved calmly but quickly. I stood with Keyan beside the bed while Karyn sat beside Haydn, her hand gently on his chest, waiting. A mixture of awe and wonder welled up inside me. Spellbound by the mystery and majesty of this moment, I sensed that I stood in a sacred place, in sacred time, not sure what it all meant but bowing my head in submission. My heart felt both indescribable relief and wrenching sorrow. We watched Haydn take his last deep breaths out and out and out. Time stood still. We whispered our love and prayers in those final precious moments as our beloved son pulled away from this earthly life. I remember reaching into the depths of what little reserves I had left to say, "Go well, beloved Haydn, go well." And then, he was gone. The chest that we had come to watch finally stilled and our beautiful braveheart's suffering was finally over. With a single step he had walked through the veil that separates us here from the immortal realm and the pavilion of eternity.

> *O SON OF LOVE!*
> *Thou art but one step away from the glorious heights above and from the celestial tree of love. Take thou one pace and with the next advance into the immortal realm and enter the pavilion of eternity.*
> —Bahá'u'lláh, *The Hidden Words*, Persian no. 7

It is an awesome and profoundly sacred gift to be able to witness the transition of a loved one taking their leave from this world, especially when the transition is peaceful and at least somewhat prepared. In my experience, having also held my beloved father in my arms as he took his last breath seven years earlier, there is nothing to compare except perhaps to witness the birth of a child into this world. The parallels are poignant. In both, there is a heightened sense of being in the presence of the sacredness of life itself. The life forces that shape all that was, all that is, and all that will be are mysteriously concentrated into a single moment. In that moment, we experience a genuine humility and awe, watching the crossing over from one world into the next. Such a crossing is rarely effortless. It can be painful, even traumatic, sometimes dangerous. Here is a moment to embrace the skills of science—especially if there is a need for intervention—and the light of faith. For anyone who is witness to such a sacred moment, our role is to be profoundly present and as calm and confident as we can be. At risk of stating the obvious, without exception, we are all created to go through birth and death. Billions of human beings, over millions of years, have taken these sacred rites of passage. It is as natural as breathing, more so perhaps, as breathing can be a choice and even stopped.

To accompany a loved one to the veil is to prepare a lover to be reunited with their true beloved in the eternal realm. In that paradise of the placeless, there is only love, and the concept of family surely expands to embrace all denizens of that kingdom. There, in the place where neither "there" nor "here," nor even "place," have meaning, even the word *family* is left behind for those of us still living in the kingdom of words. Here in the workshop that is this world, hopefully we catch a glimpse of the intimacy of love and trust that is a faint glimmering of what awaits when we are freed from the limitations of words and emotions associated with the material realm.

Rarely do we get a trial run at approaching the veil. We almost all do so for the first and only time. Even if we have been with someone else as they took their last breath, that doesn't give us any advantage or special tools when it comes to our time to transition ourselves. Haydn was a remarkably wholesome young man whose faith, trust, and fortitude enabled him to approach death without fear or anxiety. Just like all of us, he was a first-timer at taking that sacred step from this world into the next. When that time approached, his body was weak, and his brain and spinal fluid were victim to a highly aggressive tumor.

On Tuesday, May 19, I wrote the most difficult and heartrending email that I have ever written:

Dearest friends and family,

After nine and a half months since being diagnosed with a rare and aggressive brain cancer, our beloved Haydn has today been freed from his physical suffering. He passed on from this world around half past nine this morning, Tuesday 19 May, peacefully and in our home. We humbly request your prayers for the progress of his radiant soul as he continues his eternal journey towards God.

With gratitude and love, from the fragments of our broken hearts,

AdamKarynTallisSian(Haydn)Keyan

P.S. The prayer we said this morning includes a profound and moving statement: "O my God, Thy Trust hath been returned unto Thee." This is also the quotation carved into the gravestone of Haydn's youngest sibling, our beloved Xander Ali Robarts, who passed away in Beijing, China on June 24, 2008, before his tiny feet were able to touch this earth. We never expected Haydn to be the first of us to be reunited with Xander, but we can only imagine that loving embrace in heaven today.

Haydn had a deep love for his youngest brother, Xander, whom he never met in person but with whom he had a deep personal connection. When Karyn was pregnant with Xander, Haydn was eight years old. He rushed home from school to fix her ginger tea for nausea, rubbed her feet and back, and gently held her hair back when morning sickness struck. He kissed her belly to show his love for both his mother and his unborn brother. Haydn was in the room with his siblings when we accompanied Karyn to an ultrasound at five months. He was present to hear the doctor's heavy words when he asked the children to please leave the room so he could speak privately to Karyn and me. Two days later, at their request, Haydn and his siblings helped to dig the grave and inter the tiny casket that contained the precious body of their baby brother whom they never met. For years they would go to that sacred spot, a village cemetery in the mountains, to clean Xander's humble gravestone and plant *sibuliao*, traditional flowers used for graves in rural China. *Sibuliao* means "they don't die." When I think of these flowers, I am reminded of a beautiful saying that I heard during my childhood in Africa: "Africans don't die; they rise to greatness!"

In testament to his love and connection to Xander, as well as his sensitive and precise nature, Haydn designed a silver necklace engraved with a long line of numbers. Those numbers were the exact GPS coordinates of Xander's resting place, which he visited more often than anyone. One day in Toronto, Haydn said that if he made it to the next world before I did, he would be happy to embrace Xander for all of us.

reflections
on descent

To everything there is a season, and a time to every purpose under the heaven: A time to be born, and a time to die; a time to plant, and a time to pluck up that which is planted / A time to kill, and a time to heal; a time to break down, and a time to build up / A time to weep, and a time to laugh; a time to mourn, and a time to dance / A time to cast away stones, and a time to gather stones together; a time to embrace, and a time to refrain from embracing / A time to get, and a time to lose; a time to keep, and a time to cast away / A time to rend, and a time to sew; a time to keep silence, and a time to speak / A time to love, and a time to hate; a time of war, and a time of peace.

—ECCLESIASTES 3:1 (KJV)

"As many portions of time as there are, through them the sun proceeds: he who worships time as Brahman, from him time moves away very far." And thus it is said: "From time all beings flow, from time they grow; in time they obtain rest; time is visible (sun) and invisible (moments)."

—MAITRĀYAṆA-BRĀHMAṆA UPANISHAD, 6.45

Where there is love, nothing is too much trouble, and there is always time.

—BASED ON WORDS ATTRIBUTED TO 'ABDU'L-BAHÁ,
AS RECORDED IN *Portals to Freedom*

17.

TIME

"Never miss your moment!"

<hr />

THE LAST OF THE EMAILS, SENT WEDNESDAY, MAY 27—WHICH WOULD
have been Haydn's twentieth birthday—included the following post-
script by Karyn:

> *In the last month of his life, Haydn became increasingly quiet and*
> *deeply reflective. In one such moment, sitting by his bedside, I broke the*
> *silence by asking what he was thinking about. He looked at me with*
> *those big brown eyes and said. . . . "Time. How one minute we have it*
> *and the next we don't.*
> *Carpe Diem!*

A few months after I moved from the UK to China, in 1993, I was
visiting Beijing at the same time the Ministry of Construction was
holding a symposium with delegations from the Royal Institute of
British Architects, the American Institute of Architects, and the
Hong Kong Architectural Association. I was the only member of the
RIBA at the time living in China and teaching architecture at a Chinese university. It seemed serendipitous to be in Beijing that exact
weekend, and I was, therefore, invited to join the symposium as an
adjunct to the RIBA delegation. I heard of the symposium only the

night before it started, and I was unprepared. I didn't even have a suit to wear to such a high-level gathering.

Toward the end of the first day, the deputy minister of construction turned to the assembled foreign guests and asked whether anyone had any observations regarding the current teaching of architecture in Chinese universities. I was the only one present who had any experience to address this question. But I was by far the youngest guest, and I was uncertain whether I had speaking privileges. And, besides, I wasn't wearing a suit! So I said nothing. The conversation moved on. The president of the RIBA slipped a piece of paper in front of me; on it was the handwritten note: "Never miss your moment!" Haydn and his siblings have heard this story more times than they care to tell, as I feel it is such an important message.

Life itself regularly offers opportunities that may be fleeting chances for important choices, significant impacts, and deeper learning. During Haydn's journey, there were several precious moments when opportunities presented themselves, like doors opening with brilliant and unexpected timing. Thankfully, at least with some of the more obvious opportunities, we noticed and walked through those doors.

Two of the most dramatic opportunities are now quite obvious. One, you'll recall, is when, in January, the oncologists in Toronto told Haydn there was no cure. Yet a week later we landed in New York for Haydn to commence a clinical trial of high-dose chemotherapy plus stem cell rescue. What happened during those seven extraordinary days was miraculous and certainly felt like doors opening in fast succession. This included discovering a clinical trial for relapsed mixed malignant germ cell tumors that happened to be in New York, less than an hour's flight from where we were in Toronto; connecting to lead oncologists who were able to include Haydn's case at the tumor review boards of NYU and Sloan Kettering; learning that Haydn's uncle, a distinguished doctor, would be welcome to present Haydn's case by dialing in to the tumor review board;

accepting the offer from the lead doctor to include Haydn in the clinical trial at NYU Langone; and receiving an extraordinarily kind and generous offer from friends who paid for us to fly private to New York. We felt like we were sprinting to get through all those doors before they closed!

In March came the second, more obvious, opportunity. Haydn heard the prognosis from the oncologists in New York—the treatments were not working—and three days later we flew home to Ottawa. That exact night, soon after we touched down, the borders closed between Canada and the US to curtail the spread of COVID-19. We made it through a slim door opening that quickly shut behind us. Each of these two brief moments opened an opportunity for quick action that would not have been possible a day later.

When we arrived in Ottawa, it was cold. There was still quite a bit of snow on the ground, and life for Haydn was entirely indoors. As the days moved on, the sun began to shine a little more, the ice started to melt, and we talked about getting Haydn outside to enjoy some fresh air unconstrained by the walls of his bedroom or the house. Each time the suggestion came, it was a little too much of an ask, and Haydn politely declined. Then one day, unexpectedly and to our sheer delight, Haydn announced that today was the day he wanted to go outside and sit on the porch. He bundled up in his winter coat, with gloves, scarf, and woolen hat, and out we went. That image of Haydn on the porch, sitting in the rocking chair, surrounded by family and looking out over the still frozen lake, exemplified seizing the moment. Getting outside lifted everyone's hearts, not least of which Haydn's.

A week or so after that magical time sitting together on the porch, Haydn was in bed and suddenly announced that he wanted to go down to the dock. He added that he wanted to do so "Right now!" That was ten days before he left this world. He was frail and we did not even consider this a possibility. Indeed, getting to the dock required going down four wooden steps, then down another nine stone steps, then up a step to get onto the dock itself. The dock was slippery and the water icy cold. Tallis, our eldest, and I looked at each other and realized that this was a window, a precious opportunity that might not come again, and we simply had to go for it. Haydn wasn't giving us any alternatives. So we positioned ourselves on either side of Haydn, lifted him as he put his arms around our shoulders, and we walked together. We could not put a foot wrong, yet the photos of this maneuver show us smiling and executing the steps with ease, as if we had practiced for months. We sat on the dock with Haydn beaming in joy and achievement. I took the chance to take a selfie with all six of us together. It was no professional photograph, for sure, but it was our last complete family photo. Some opportunities come occasionally, others come rarely, and some come only once. Never miss your moment!

I wonder whether some of these more spontaneous choices come from the creative right brain or the more rational left brain. Is the choice from conscious reasoning or more subconscious intuition? Haydn had a well-trained mind for sure, but the unexpected announcement that day felt more like an impulse or was prompted by an intuition that this was the moment, and it had to be seized. In the writings of Bahá'u'lláh there is a delightful and intriguing call to "ponder in thy heart." One normally associates pondering with a function of the brain, but the role of intuition, which seems like informed promptings of the heart, is often a source of great insight.

—◊—

One of Haydn's brothers likes to remind us of the importance of not living in the past or being overly focused on the future. He is right, and this issue emerged in several conversations during Haydn's journey. The day Haydn rode the train from Ottawa to Toronto to get the MRI that revealed his brain tumor happened to be the day he was to take his driving test. At this point, his vision was more blurred, sometimes even double vision, and he experienced severe headaches. While Haydn prepared for his driving test, we talked about the skills of a good driver. He would watch the rear-view mirror, side mirrors, and be able at any time during the test to not only keep a safe distance behind the car in front but also know which car was behind and how far behind. As experienced drivers, we know that most wouldn't really know the answer to those questions. I asked a friend, many years ago, who did an advanced driving test in Manchester, which nugget he thought distinguished advanced driving from normal driving. His answer was that a good driver is present to the immediate vicinity of their car, knowing how to handle the car in relation to the cars fifty feet in front and behind, as well as to the left and right. But an advanced driver also watches the road and cars five hundred feet ahead and behind. To be acutely aware of the *here* while simultaneously extending our awareness to *there* is not an either/or. Being in the present but also having one's eyes on the future and on the past is possible not only when driving a car but also in the drive through life.

Reflecting on the meaning of the moment, I became aware that this moment was not something only to be measured in seconds or minutes, nor even to be located in Toronto or New York. For sure, the moment existed in time and space, yet it was also a moment in the history of learning. In physics the word *moment* is used to describe the leverage of a force acting at a distance on an object. I realized that our moment, in terms of Haydn's journey as an episode, was also a physics moment of learning in that it could inspire others and profoundly affect their lives. Hence, seizing the moment and writing this book!

—⚍—

My current understanding is that time doesn't exist except as a useful organizing construct of the human mind. It is useful insofar as it helps order and make sense of who we are, because we can place ourselves in a context of where we are coming from and where we are going. It is, of course, beyond the scope of this book to explore the science of time or the nature of the space-time continuum that is a subject of theoretical physics. Suffice to say, though, some of the most brilliant scientists of the past two hundred years—including Newton, Einstein, Hawking, to name only some—have considered, with differing degrees of conviction, that it is not entirely delusional to posit a reality that does not need to be defined or bound by time, or by space, or by space-time.

There are increasing overlaps between the frontiers of theoretical physics and the reflections of the mystics. Each of the world's great religions—including Hinduism, Buddhism, Judaism, Christianity, Islam, and the Bahá'í Faith—include mystical teachings pertaining to the unknown and the unknowable. They all variously describe the heart of religion as the mystic bond that unites each human soul with its creator, also with an afterlife that is essentially the continued life of the human spirit, unbound by the material body it has left behind on graduation from the world of dust. And in that afterlife, in whichever language or faith tradition it is described, the human soul transcends time and space, at least as we know them here. Put more simply, time and space as we define and experience them here on earth may well be a product of the human mind to make sense of the reality here. When the human soul moves on from this world, crossing the veil that separates this world from the next, time and space may be left behind, or experienced in different attributes and manifestation befitting that world.

Although scientists can measure the passage of time very precisely, most would agree that we still have little idea what time is. Like most humans, I have been programmed to think of time in terms of beginnings and endings. This applies to daily routines, work, holidays, to life itself, even to the creation of the universe. When we think of a creator and a creation, we usually think of the creator preexisting the creation, one coming before the other in terms of time. The idea of a creator without a creation is like a king without a kingdom. In terms of cause and effect, we say that cause precedes effect, or that the creator precedes the creation, but this need not translate into a relationship in time where there is a creator without a creation. Just as we can imagine the two continuing forward into eternity, they can also have existed from eternity, albeit in different form to the creation we see today. I wonder whether this may be what is alluded to in the statement by Bahá'u'lláh in describing the Bahá'í Faith as "the changeless faith of God, eternal in the past, eternal in the future." That hardly qualifies then as a new religion! Yet, that was how I described it before I started reading the actual texts when I was nineteen.

We are also conditioned to think of time in relation to the sun. Hence, a year is the time taken for earth to orbit the sun, and a day is the time of one earth rotation. Now consider the perspective of the sun. Yesterday, today, tomorrow do not exist in the sun. Perhaps this helps to comprehend that the past, the present, and the future are coexistent—or nonexistent—in relation to God.

Accompanying Haydn through cancer offered ample opportunity to reflect upon our relationship. We are father and son. In relationship to time, I was born before he was, and he died before me. However, I believe the reality of our relationship transcends these constructs of time. Our relationship is one of companionship, understanding, love, respect, and trust. Therefore, there is no reason it should be limited by time or space. The bonds are spiritual, and they don't perish just because our bodies perish. Indeed, the reality of the afterlife is the continuity of our spiritual lives. This world is our studio to develop spiritual qualities and virtues, and our material human body is the vehicle we use to transport us through. To turn the vehicle into an idol, or its development into the goal, risks missing the more fundamental purpose of life. When that purpose is spiritual growth, then time becomes of less consequence, for, as we read in the quotes at the beginning of this chapter, "There is always time."

—៣—

Another question Haydn pondered during his journey was his life's service to humanity. In his notebook, and on more than one occasion when we were together, Haydn openly shared that before his journey through cancer, he hoped to lead a life of service *after* first building a foundation—degrees, family, material security—so that he would be in a strong position to give to others, serve them, and make contributions to the betterment of the world. He said that one of his most poignant lessons from his cancer journey was that one does not have to wait to be fit to serve. The best way to become mountain fit is to get on the mountain. We can live lives of service to others with every breath we take. The mountains are ever present. The time is always now.

In Haydn's words:

> *Before I thought to truly give back, I thought I had to have at least enough financial freedom that I could live in comfort while "giving" . . . but that's not the point. What's stopping you from doing so now?*
>
> *Cancer has forced me to reevaluate that plan that I had made for myself . . . none of us truly know how much time we have so none of us can truly determine "when" is that perfect time to start giving. It doesn't have to be financially, in fact it SHOULDN'T be primarily financially in how we give back . . . start with what you can do . . . put a smile on people's faces, bring joy to people's lives . . . it will make their day that little bit better.*
>
> *"We should be like the fountain constantly giving of itself." ('Abdu'l-Bahá)*

In the same email with which we started this chapter, Karyn's words continued:

> *Time. As this word swirls in my mind, my heart turns to a poignant and beautiful quote by Bahá'u'lláh, where He says: "Dedicate the*

precious days of your life to the betterment of the world." Although Haydn was deeply grateful for his life, and graciously accepted his death, he still wanted to do more to make the world a better place. God willing, we will do that for him, in our own way, in our own time.

Wishing to establish his own character, he also establishes the character of others, and wishing to be prominent himself, he also helps others to be prominent.

—ANALECTS OF CONFUCIUS, 6.28

In the same way that the essence of man is the soul, the soul of this world is the subtle growth of spirituality, heavenly morals, divine favors, and sacred powers. Were the physical world not accompanied by this spirit, it could not exist.

—'ABDU'L-BAHÁ, *Divine Philosophy*, 3.32

The best of wisdom what is accompanied by work.

—IMAM ALI, *2500 Adages of Imam Ali*, 4.136

18.

ACCOMPANIMENT

"Mutual aid and reciprocity."

————————————

WITH CANCER SPREADING IN HIS SPINAL CORD AND AFFECTING HIS nerves, it was likely only a matter of time before Haydn would not be able to walk. Yet he wanted so desperately to move on his own that we did whatever we could to support his walking, including procuring a walker that allowed much of his weight to be taken on his forearms. Ten days before he passed away, Haydn took his last steps as he walked to the dining room. Sadly, on this dreaded day, Haydn's legs collapsed beneath him. As Haydn fell to his knees, I partially cushioned his fall, as I was right behind him. With the two of us on our knees, on the floor, there was no shouting, screaming, or blaming. Haydn simply and calmly said, "Get the wheelchair." We lifted him into the wheelchair and proceeded to the dining table, where he ate heartily. That was the last real meal he ate with us.

When someone who is frail or unwell feels weak, they naturally want to feel strong and capable. So when we do things for them that they can do for themselves, it is not an act of support but of disempowerment. Regardless of the intention, we take away their joy in being able to do something that should still be theirs to do. Learning how to accompany a weaker person rather than to just do for them is not usually a skill we learn in schools or in many families—especially in the frenetic family life of our fast-paced and materially advanced urban societies. So where and how do we learn true accompaniment? And, without at least some of the key skills of accompaniment, how can we expect to be capable parents and mountain guides, especially of older children who are clearly able to do much on their own? For nineteen-year-olds, the nourishing parenting they received as a child swiftly becomes patronizing and disempowering, even when they become frail.

I remember being advised that if one is having a conversation with a teenager, it is far more effective to be shoulder to shoulder, rather than face to face. That is a simple gesture that creates a sense of looking in the same direction rather than looking in opposite directions. It is a shift to looking *with* each other rather than *at* each other. Accompaniment is an art whose mastery I believe would greatly assist relationships of many varieties: family, friends, workplaces, communities, and even countries. At the risk of being over simplistic, relationships that apply mutual accompaniment as their modus operandi are relationships that walk side by side toward a common goal, finding solutions in togetherness rather than otherness.

The concept of accompaniment has been familiar in the psychology field since the late 1960s. It gained traction with liberation theology, notably in Latin America, through the Peruvian priest Gustavo Gutiérrez, who wrote *A Theology of Liberation*, one of the movement's defining books addressing the plight of the marginalized through elevating their rightful roles in civic and political affairs. Interestingly, the root of the Spanish *acompañamiento* is *compañero* or friend. It derives from the Latin *ad cum panis*, which means to break bread with one another.

With this influence, Paul Farmer, department chair of Global Health and Social Medicine at Harvard Medical School and founder of Partners in Health, went on to designate accompaniment as the cornerstone of his practice. In his 2013 book, *To Repair the World: Paul Farmer Speaks to the Next Generation*, he states:

> *To accompany someone is to go somewhere with him or her, to break*

bread together, to be on a journey together with a beginning and an end. There's an element of mystery, of openness, of trust in accompaniment. The companion, or accompagnateur, *says: "I'll go with you and support you on your journey wherever it leads. I'll share your fate for a while—and by 'a while'—I don't mean a little while." Accompaniment is about sticking with a task until it's deemed completed—not by the* accompagnateur *but by the one being accompanied.*[1]

In a 2015 article in the *Journal of Social and Political Psychology*, Mary Watkins shares insightful research on the role of the accompanier. She explains, "For the accompanier, accompaniment steers us toward a different kind of being-present. . . . It moves away from forms of egoic rationality that support control, management, 'fixing,' and 'intervening.' . . . The accompanier brings his presence to what is difficult, allowing it to affect him, to matter to him, to alter his course."[2] Watkins notes that *accompaniment* is a term currently used in social medicine, peace activism, human rights, pastoral support, and social and liberation psychology.

It is increasingly apparent that the art of accompaniment relates to how close one truly becomes to another in ways that convey support, solidarity, mutual empowerment, and greater understanding. As pioneering lawyer/activist Bryan Stevenson so powerfully articulates in his writing and speaking and in the documentary *True Justice*, which followed his work with the Equal Justice Initiative, we have to "get proximate" with the issues of our time if we wish to meaningfully understand or begin to solve them. That applies to dealing with injustice and dealing with disease. One can meaningfully address poverty only if one has met a person in poverty; COVID-19 researchers could find a vaccine only by getting proximate to the virus; one can achieve holistic wellness and healing by getting proximate to one's inner and outer being.

In their book, *St. Francis and the Foolishness of God*, Marie Dennis and Cynthia Moe-Lobeda describe accompaniment as "to deviate from other pathways for a while (and then forever), to walk with those on the margins, to be with them, to let go. Accompaniment is an idea so radical and difficult for us to comprehend that its power and significance reveal themselves to our Western and Northern minds only slowly and with great difficulty."[3]

My experience accompanying Haydn on his journey through cancer led me to consider accompaniment at four levels. At the basic level, it is being in the same space, whether literal or virtual, with the person we accompany. According to a Brazilian proverb, "the head thinks from where the feet are planted." At the next level, we get proximate in that same space, effectively removing any barrier between us, to eliminate any sense of "them" and "us." Instead of being together conversing across a fence, there is no fence. At the third level, one moves from just being together to *doing* together—the metaphorical breaking of bread together and sharing. At the fourth level of accompaniment, we begin to walk together on a path of service to others. We hold back from leading when it is paramount that others do. We co-create knowledge and share it with others. Now accompaniment becomes truly mutual and an extension beyond the person accompanying and the person accompanied. I personally believe that this type of accompaniment is not limited to this earthly life, as it has such a significant spiritual aspect.

—⚬⚬—

One night, about five weeks before Haydn left us, the two of us sat on the edge of his bed, eating waffles with berry compote. It was 3:00 a.m., and the house was quiet. I looked across at Haydn and my heart spoke out loud. "I wish I could go with you," I said. Haydn smiled and asked me if I would like to finish his waffle.

I struggled to adequately learn how a good climbing guide accompanies a climber on the slog. My natural tendency would be to carry my climber all the way to the summit, if needed. This may be an easy-way-out option for both guide and climber. Would this "helping" be an act of selfishness by the guide, avoiding the discomfort of watching another struggle? Is this truly guiding? For a climber, would opting for such ease no longer make them a climber? Any guide offering to carry their climbers would in effect be stealing their feeling of momentous triumph that stems from struggle and discovering their own abilities, while negating the seeking that brought them to the mountain in the first place. Mountaineering friend and writer Karen Malmqvist reminds her climb teams that "we are only as strong as our weakest link, and every day that link may change. One day, it may be you." I've learned that best guiding practices embody the importance of making decisions by placing oneself in another's boots.

While I have used the metaphor of the climber and climbing guide to describe how Haydn and I worked together, the truth is there *were* times we swapped roles. Haydn might turn to me and say, "Time to breathe!" or he would prepare a workout schedule for me to use at the gym in the condo we rented in Toronto. Other times, too many to number, there were no labels, no roles—we were just companions on a shared journey. Those were perhaps the most precious of our times in the nine and a half months from Haydn's diagnosis to his eventual graduation from this world. They were often times of no seeming importance, at least as far as the journey was concerned, but they were among the most treasured of all our times. In those final weeks at the lake house, Haydn would wake at least a couple of times each night. Sitting beside Haydn on the edge of his bed on those occasions, we leaned in together to that spiritual space where labels merge and become irrelevant. It may have been the dead of night and very quiet in the house, but we scaled the heights of steep slopes on the edge of life itself. Memorable moments, indeed.

—ᴟ—

Some months after Haydn's passing, I shared Haydn's story with Karen Malmqvist. She reminded me that mountain climbing comprises both the ascent and the descent. Descending the mountain, one's pack is lighter, as one is carrying less weight—both literally and figuratively. She mentioned Joseph Campbell's story line of the hero's journey, in which the hero returns home to tell the story of the climb, to share the elixir of new knowledge gained for the betterment of all. As she pointed this out, the clarity became obvious. It was I who had, in fact, been the mountaineer with the good fortune to make this climb and return to tell this story. As tears welled up in my eyes, I realized that I had been given the priceless bounty of having Haydn as *my* mountain guide. Without Haydn, and his heroic sacrifice of giving his all to get us to the mountain summit, I would have been stuck in my life, believing that I knew something about mountains but without having made the climb.

19.

AFTERWORD

ONE DAY, HAYDN TURNED TO KARYN AND SAID, "MOM, I HAVE HAD such a wonderful life, so full of opportunities and privileges. Nothing has prepared me for this." He was well aware that his first major climb was Himalayan in scope, and he was being tested to his capacity.

It was a terrible loss for our family when Haydn passed away on May 19, 2020. No prior education or experience had taught us how to grieve, and grief can be an overpowering mountain of its own. We quickly realized that different people, and certainly different cultures, even within one family, grieve differently. This was a powerful test of our abilities to validate one another's feelings and experiences rather than trying to mold them to match our own. For me, it was a second round of learning to accompany rather than direct. Realizing that this test was back helped me see that I had not adequately mastered it in my role as a climber on Haydn's team.

In his inauguration speech as president of South Africa, delivered on May 10, 1994, Nelson Mandela remarked on the never-ending journey of human freedom. Although in a different context than Haydn's mountain, Mandela's famous statement resonates:

I have discovered the secret that after climbing a great hill, one only finds that there are many more hills to climb. I have taken a moment here to rest, to steal a view of the glorious vista that surrounds me, to look back on the distance I have come. But I can rest only for a moment, for with freedom comes responsibilities, and I dare not linger, for my long walk is not yet ended.[1]

What lies ahead? That question is often foremost in our minds, and some would advocate that we make specific plans for the future and then make those plans work, sometimes at all costs. That approach can work for some, and there are plenty of self-help books and talks that would point us in such a direction. But such an approach can also distract us from living in the present and being grateful for what we have now. This dichotomy can be solved by the simple realization that we live in the presence of a divine and all-loving power, the omnipotent, omnipresent, omniscient creator of all that has been and all that will be, including each one of us unique beings.

In the language of science, all the laws of the universe testify to what we can and can't do. In the language of faith, "All are His servants, and all abide by His bidding." Living in such presence, with divine love in our hearts, and reinforced with the power of His Name, we can joyfully take each breath, one at a time, as we confidently and humbly ascend, one step at a time, the mountains before us. No mountain is too great, no summit too high. As Haydn demonstrated through dying with grace and gratitude, and as we can show through living with grace and gratitude, we can "take one step and with the next enter the pavilion of eternity."

—⁓—

Today I received a call from a dear friend who knows our family well. He read our email updates and could tell that this was the fruit of a father's love for his son. He called to say that he no longer saw the emails as rose tinted; that Haydn really was an unusually pure soul.

My response: every soul is created pure and noble. Alas, it is our poor parenting, our confused societal messages, our self-centered educational systems, our degrading media, our manipulated politics, our outmoded religions, our morally bankrupt leadership, in short, our world order that makes for a tarnished result. How can one swim in sewage and stay clean? Haydn had a concerted go at trying to be authentic, caring, kind, generous, and thoughtful of others. Ironically, this kind, thoughtful, selfless giant was afflicted with a terminal disease and was unable to survive it, despite his very best efforts and the best medical care we could find. In his last months, Haydn felt he became stronger, his faith became clearer, and he felt contentment.

Haydn also became more, rather than less, hopeful for the world's future. That was most poignantly clear from his letter to Keyan. Haydn's journey is a story of faith, hope, love, and, above all, the mystery of suffering. If his example gives hope to others, then this book will have served its purpose. And all that suffering—those endless pokes and prods in so many hospitals, the nausea and sometimes excruciating pain, the push to the limits of what he could bear—will not have been wasted. Instead, like the heat in the story of the refiner of silver, it will have helped purify, clarify, and reflect the beauty and nobility that is the innate birthright of every human being. In the end it is these spiritual qualities that make us uniquely human, for only human beings can make the conscious choice to be noble beings. We make that choice not once but with every breath we take. And, as with mountain climbing, it is a defining journey, often challenging, unknown, tiring, and sometimes painful. But, also like mountain climbing, it is full of increasing wonderment, learning, achievement, and joy.

I don't know many nineteen-year-olds who write wills; but Haydn wrote his will before he left this world. He didn't have much by way of material possessions or wealth to allocate, and in fact there is no mention of anything like that in the document. Instead, he passed on his wishes. At the top of the list was the following:

Live a life filled with joy and try to consciously consider how to bring joy to the lives of those around you as well.

I have read and reread that sentence many times since Haydn's passing. Every time I do, one word keeps jumping out at me: *consciously*. Looking back on my life before Haydn's journey of suffering, it feels to me that I lived in a relatively unconscious or semiconscious state. This journey became a real wake-up call—to notice more, love more, be more conscious of the bounties that are raining down upon every one of us at every moment. In chapter 14, we recalled Haydn's childhood wish that he might die "saving somebody's life." In the end, it seems he did, in many ways.

This was a classic hero's journey through unfamiliar terrain, with its fair share of dragons and scary slopes. It required us to be on our toes, to be mindful of our steps and of each other's steps. It was a call to accept risks and witness wonders. It was a lesson in conquering fear through reliance on the deepest bonds of love and trust. And, like any hero's journey, one returns to the world to tell the story and share the learning and wonder with others.

So we realize that this book is more than a memoir. Or a self-help book. Or a spiritual guide. As a unique blend, inspired by a unique individual, it is an approach book, sharing an approach to life, an approach to the mountains unique to each of us but shared by all of us. After all, it's Haydn's approach to living and dying that inspires these nineteen lessons.

—◊—

After Haydn passed away, his mother found the following note in Haydn's little black notebook that he kept beside his bed:

I don't want people to disrupt their lives grieving. . . keep working, keep loving, keep smiling, keep contributing to the community and to the cause, and remember me with a nice haircut, not bald ;)

I want to be a beacon of joy and happiness, whether alive or in the next world . . . please fulfill this wish for me if I am unable to do so myself . . . try whenever you can to bring a smile to people's faces, to be a light in a dark room, so do what you can to help others.

NOTES

CHAPTER 2

1. "Chi de ku zhong ku, fang wei ren shang ren" 吃尽苦中苦，方为人上人.
2. Brett Q. Ford et al., "The Psychological Health Benefits of Accepting Negative Emotions and Thoughts: Laboratory, Diary, and Longitudinal Evidence," *Journal of Personality and Social Psychology* 115, no. 6 (December 2018): 1075–92, www.ncbi.nlm.nih.gov/pmc/articles/PMC5767148/.

CHAPTER 3

1. For an excellent critique of competition, see *No Contest: The Case Against Competition* by Alfie Kohn; also *Beyond the Culture of Contest: From Adversarialism to Mutualism in an Age of Interdependence* by Michael Karlberg.
2. See Suleika Jaouad's memoir, *Between Two Kingdoms: A Memoir of a Life Interrupted* (New York: Random House, 2021). Also, Suleika Jaouad at TED 2019 "What Almost Dying Taught Me about Living."
3. Jennifer Beer, "The Inconvenient Truth about Your 'Authentic' Self," *Scientific American Blog Network*, March 5, 2020, blogs.scientificamerican.com/observations/the-inconvenient-truth-about-your-authentic-self/.
4. Ibid.

CHAPTER 4

1. Martin E. P. Seligman and Mihaly Csikszentmihalyi, "Positive Psychology: An Introduction," *American Psychologist*, January 2000, p. 7.

CHAPTER 5

1. Václav Havel, *Disturbing the Peace: A Conversation with Karel Hvížd'ala* (New York: Vintage Books, 1991), 181.
2. Ibid., 181–82.

CHAPTER 6

1. 'Abdu'l-Bahá, *Bahá'í World Faith*, 87.1. 'Abdu'l-Bahá (1844–1921) was the eldest son of Bahá'u'lláh (1817–1892), who was the founder of the Bahá'í Faith. Like his father, 'Abdu'l-Bahá spent most of his life as a

prisoner of the Persian and Ottoman empires, until his release in 1908. His subsequent travels to Europe and North America were instrumental in bringing the Bahá'í Faith to the attention of a Western audience and to promoting its core teaching of world unity.

CHAPTER 8

1. Al Gore, *Earth in the Balance: Ecology and Human Spirit* (New York: Houghton Mifflin, 1992).
2. Alí Nakhjavání (September 19, 1919–October 11, 2019).

CHAPTER 10

1. 'Abdu'l-Bahá, *Selections from the Writings of 'Abdu'l-Bahá*, 169.2.
2. Gideon Lichfield, "The Science of Near-Death Experiences," *The Atlantic*, November 23, 2015, www.theatlantic.com/magazine/archive /2015/04/the-science-of-near-death-experiences/386231/.
3. Eckhart Tolle, https://members.eckharttolle.com/video/what-is-the -difference-between-intuition-and-fear/.

CHAPTER 13

1. 'Abdu'l-Bahá, *Paris Talks*, 36.3.
2. Rainn Wilson, USC Baccalaureate Speech 2014, https://www.youtube .com/watch?v=AnjGSsmgz8Q.
3. Brother David Steindl-Rast and Sharon Lebell, *Music of Silence: A Sacred Journey Through the Hours of the Day* (Berkeley: Ulysses Press, 2001).
4. "Rabindranath Tagore Quotes," *BrainyQuote*, Xplore, www.brainyquote .com/quotes/rabindranath_tagore_134933.

CHAPTER 14

1. https://www.ted.com/talks/abigail_marsh_why_some_people_are _more_altruistic_than_others/transcript?language=en.
2. Ibid.

CHAPTER 16

1. Bahá'í International Community, *Valuing Spirituality in Development, February 18, 1998.*

CHAPTER 18

1. Paul Farmer, *To Repair the World: Paul Farmer Speaks to the Next Generation* (Berkeley: University of California Press, 2019).
2. Mary Watkins, "Psychosocial Accompaniment," *Journal of Social and Political Psychology* 3, no. 1 (August 2015): 324–41, jspp.psychopen.eu /index.php/jspp/article/download/4861/4861.html?inline=1.

3. Marie Dennis et al., *St. Francis and the Foolishness of God* (Maryknoll, NY: Orbis Books, 2015).

CHAPTER 19

1. "Nelson Mandela's Inaugural Address as President of South Africa," 1994, www.blackpast.org/global-african-history/1994-nelson-mandela -s-inaugural-address-president-south-africa/.

ACKNOWLEDGMENTS

THE FIRST ACKNOWLEDGMENT MUST BE HAYDN HIMSELF. I AM IN AWE OF his inspiring example, of so many of the qualities that are described in the chapters of this book. I hope that these pages may in some humble way be a befitting tribute to his short but remarkable life.

Climbers derive great support from the other members of the climb team, and Haydn and I were certainly not alone. A huge debt of gratitude goes to the medical professionals who took care of Haydn in Toronto, New York, and Ottawa. They are not only the selfless and hardworking nurses and world-class doctors but also the technically brilliant people who worked often late at night running the CT scans or the MRI machines, the blood labs, the hospital kitchens, and porters who drove gurneys along endless corridors between inpatient rooms and imaging departments for seemingly endless orders.

True friendship knows no bounds. I would like to acknowledge and thank Haydn's friends who supported him to the very end through their calls and messages, mostly on Instagram and Snapchat. Some traveled from other cities, countries, and even continents, to visit even if Haydn was too weak to spend more than an hour or so with them. Some of those friends pulled all-nighters, sitting at Haydn's bedside in the hospital, just to be there.

Throughout this book I have inserted segments of communications received from friends of Haydn's and ours—this journey would have been impossible without them, and I am grateful for their permission to include these inspirational messages.

Haydn's family, from seven countries and four continents, poured their love and generosity into this journey. No climber could have wished for a more devoted team of support, whether from young nephews and nieces, or grandmothers and great-grandmothers. I would dearly like to mention everyone by name, however, there have been too many who joined the support team on this journey. You know who you are and know that no words could ever adequately express the depth of gratitude our family feels. To every one of you, thank you!

If there is one person who must be mentioned by name, it is undoubtedly my wife, Karyn. To ask any mother to watch her nineteen-year-old son fight a losing battle with a terminal disease over a nine-and-a-half-month course is unthinkable. It is nothing short of miraculous that Karyn remained so calm and collected, so loving and positive. Of course, her secret was that she didn't see Haydn's cancer as a losing battle. She didn't even see it as a battle. For Karyn, it was the current chapter in her journey of unconditional love for her beloved son, in which every moment was to be lived and treasured to the full.

Fortunately, authors have the right to acknowledge more than one person by name. We couldn't have navigated this journey without the loving, skillful, resourceful, and highly knowledgeable support of my brother, Dr. Simon Robarts, and his personal researcher and wife, Andrea. If I was Haydn's climbing companion, then Simon was mine—only his pack included a brilliant medical knowledge and skill set . . . perfectly equipped for this type of climb!

Thanks to Professor Tarrant Mahony, a dear family friend, for his encouragement and wisdom, also his calls with Haydn as he navigated the marvelous world of dreams—the subject of one of my favorite chapters.

For a first-time author, I owe a particular debt of gratitude to Karen Malmqvist, who worked with me on the manuscript through all its phases as an experienced writer and mountaineer. Her guidance was invaluable and her name on the cover is well earned. I am very grateful to Paul Wright for his work as legal counsel for Team Nineteen and for introducing me to literary giants Peter Miller and Lou Aronica, who agreed to be my respective agent and editor. Peter led this book's journey to market and Lou masterfully curated the writing so that Haydn's story and its lessons remain in the spotlight. Peter also put the lessons in this book to the ultimate test, as he himself suffered through his own cancer treatments, eventually winging his flight from this world on August 20, 2021. Although Peter never physically met Haydn, he developed a deep bond of affection with Haydn's spirit and often said that he felt Haydn's close companionship and support, being "on his shoulder." Thank you to Sarah Robarts and her team at Ballantines PR for believing in this book and championing it, especially during a time when so many authors write about the tragedy of loss. Finally, I am humbled that Judith Regan, CEO of Regan Arts, quickly saw that *Nineteen* is a book with potential to positively impact a world besieged by suffering and an overwhelming fear of death. It is an honor that *Nineteen* is the launch publication for LEO, Regan's new imprint. I am profoundly grateful to have landed a publisher with the courage, confidence, and audacity to bring this story and its message to your hands and, hopefully, your hearts.

A book about spiritual climbing should probably also acknowledge the mountain itself. In this case the terrain we navigated was a journey through cancer. But the rules of climbing, and the lessons learned from this particular climb, apply to many other journey types, whether illness or loss, or a myriad of other obstacles. The key is that it *is* a climb. The steeper the mountain, the greater its challenges, the more lessons it may likely offer.

During the nine and a half months of this journey, and in the grief that followed, I listened to podcasts and TED talks too numerous to count, and I read a number of books that likely had an influence on my thoughts and reflections. I read books by Allan Watts, Eckhart Tolle, Michael Singer, Jon Kabat-Zinn, Harold S. Kushner, Thich Nhat Hanh, to name some. I continued my habit of reading from the holy books of the world's religions, especially the Bahá'í Faith, which constitutes the most modern of these.

ACKNOWLEDGMENTS

If there are insights in this book that reflect such influences, I hope these have been quoted or paraphrased without misrepresentation. In the end, I have tried to make the words here my own, but I do not wish to claim uniqueness or credit for any insights that are not my own. If you read these pages and hear an echo, especially if it rings true, then that is wonderful. Hopefully, it is an echo that resonates and inspires, maybe even prompting a return to reading the wisdom of sages and source material that is as heartwarming and soul nourishing as I found it to be.

ABOUT THE AUTHORS

ADAM ROBARTS was born in London and raised in Uganda and Kenya. He returned to the UK to study architecture at Cambridge University. Adam and his wife, Karyn, went on to establish an award-winning design firm in China. They have four children, who were all born and raised in Beijing.

In December 2018, during a family vacation in Canada, Adam was asked what he would choose to be if he were not an architect. He replied without hesitation, "A hospice nurse." Five years earlier, he had a profound experience accompanying his father through the final weeks of life before he died of cancer in Uganda. Adam could not have imagined then that nine months later he would begin to accompany his nineteen-year-old son, Haydn, through a battle with a rare brain cancer. Haydn graduated from this physical world in May 2020, one week before his twentieth birthday.

Nineteen, Adam's first book, shares the beautiful and poignant lessons learned on his family's journey with Haydn.

—ᴍ—

KAREN MALMQVIST is a recognized journalist, photographer, and public speaker. She has led her own public relations and strategic development firm, and has written for and advised leaders of nations as well as Fortune 500 companies around the world. She is the co-founder of the nonprofit *live it up!*, an adventure-based leadership program that seeks to empower women. Karen is fascinated by the limitless power of the human spirit and what people can achieve when they open up their potential. She is a high-altitude mountaineer, avid cyclist, and novice surfer. She approaches life with passion, purpose, and joy.

LOU ARONICA collaborated with Sir Ken Robinson on the *New York Times* bestsellers *The Element* and *Finding Your Element*, and with Jim Kwik on the recent *New York Times* bestseller *Limitless*. Lou is also the coauthor of the nonfiction bestseller *The Culture Code* with Clotaire Rapaille, and *The Greatest You* with Trent Shelton. He is the author of national bestselling novels *The Forever Year, Blue, The Journey Home*, and *When You Went Away*. He is the President and Publisher of the independent publishing house The Story Plant, and a past president of Novelists, Inc.

THANK YOU

It brings me great pleasure to know that you are holding Nineteen in your hands. Its journey from concept to completion has been a labor of love. I hope these pages will bring you much thought and joy.

These days, publishing success relies heavily on endorsements, especially in social media. I encourage you to share your feedback and to give Nineteen a shout-out after you have read the book. Let's together make this a contribution to one of our generation's most helpful & meaningful conversations.

Our Instagram: nineteen.book

Thank you!